Katia and Tim Carter

Cambridge IGCSE®
Core English as a Second Language
Coursebook

CAMBRIDGE
UNIVERSITY PRESS

CAMBRIDGE
UNIVERSITY PRESS

University Printing House, Cambridge CB2 8BS, United Kingdom

One Liberty Plaza, 20th Floor, New York, NY 10006, USA

477 Williamstown Road, Port Melbourne, VIC 3207, Australia

314–321, 3rd Floor, Plot 3, Splendor Forum, Jasola District Centre, New Delhi – 110025, India

103 Penang Road, #05-06/07, Visioncrest Commercial, Singapore 238467

Cambridge University Press is part of the University of Cambridge.

It furthers the University's mission by disseminating knowledge in the pursuit of education, learning and research at the highest international levels of excellence.

www.cambridge.org

First published 2015

20 19 18 17 16 15 14 13 12 11

Printed in Poland by Opolgraf

A catalogue record for this publication is available from the British Library

ISBN 978-1-107-51566-6 Paperback Student's Book With Audio CD

Contents

Menu

Introduction

The *Cambridge IGCSE® Core English as a Second Language* Coursebook is for students who are new to study at this level. The book provides a detailed introduction to all the tasks for the four key skills: reading, speaking, listening and writing. It also provides language sections focusing on vocabulary, grammar and pronunciation to improve students' general level of English. You will be guided through the skills based tasks, taught how to approach each of them, and given a lot of opportunity for practice.

By the end of the course you will have learnt:

*   how to complete various language tasks
*   to use techniques which will help you improve your language performance in all four skills
*   what the most common mistakes are and how to avoid them.

By the end of the course you will also have:

*   practised all four skills through a wide range of tasks
*   learnt a variety of authentic everyday English expressions
*   become more fluent and accurate when using your English in speaking and writing
*   learnt to assess your own progress and to identify your strengths and weaknesses
*   to become a more independent learner.

The book is divided into ten chapters. Each chapter is based round an engaging and stimulating topic. The chapters are made up of sections which focus on all four skills, as well as providing language input to help you express your ideas more clearly and accurately. In the language sections you will be encouraged to analyse grammar and vocabulary first and then practise it in a range of activities. At the end of each vocabulary and language focus section, you will find a productive task called 'Activate your English'. These 'Activate your English' tasks have been carefully designed so that while doing the activity you will also be using the target language you have learnt in that section. This will ensure that you gain more confidence when using real English.

In addition to these main sections, you can also find the following features:

Objectives – these inform you about what each section in that chapter deals with and what you will have learnt by the time you have finished the chapter. These sections inform you about the main focus of each chapter:

a   skills – reading, speaking, listening and writing

b   language skills – focusing on accuracy

c   an 'Activate your English' section – focusing on fluency practice.

Projects – these are extra activities to provide research opportunities on the topic of the reading section. You will be asked to have a discussion about what you find out, deliver a talk, or prepare a poster with information for others to look at. You will also conduct surveys of other students' opinions on certain topics. Most projects are followed by a whole class discussion on the issues raised, or by a written task. These extra writing tasks take the form of formal letters and reports.

Study tips – these sections suggest ways in which you can become a more successful and independent learner.

Key terms – these sections will give you explanations of some of the language terms used in the book.

'Did you know?' – these boxes contain interesting facts about the topics in each chapter.

Summary: 'Can you remember …?' – these pages give you the opportunity to check how much you can remember about what you have learnt in that chapter.

Progress checks – these sections allow you to examine your own learning and progress more critically. You will be asked to look back at the Objectives at the beginning of the chapter, assess your own learning and identify your strengths and weaknesses. This will assist you in putting together your own personalised revision timetable. It will help you decide which areas you need to look at when revising.

We hope you will find this book helpful and enjoy using it as much as we enjoyed writing it. We wish you happy learning.

Katia and Tim Carter

Chapter 1:
People of the world

Objectives

In this chapter, you will learn and practise:

- reading skills – answering questions about greetings from around the world
- speaking skills – discussing the topic of 'Good manners' and developing ideas
- listening skills – listening to four short recordings and answering questions
- writing skills – writing an informal letter/email that gives advice.

You will also learn and practise the following language skills:

- vocabulary of greetings
- giving advice
- making suggestions.

You will 'Activate your English' by:

- giving advice through role-play.

📖 Reading

Pre-reading activity

Greetings

Look at the photographs and discuss what greetings they show.

Do you know what countries these greetings are from?

Do you know any other unusual greetings? Tell each other what they are.

💬 Vocabulary 1

Look at the following six phrases and match them to the correct photograph. If you are not sure of the meaning, use an English dictionary. If you do not have an

Key term: scanning

Scanning is a reading technique which involves looking through a text quickly to find words, phrases or numbers that you need to answer questions. It is like looking up words in a dictionary.

English dictionary, try one of the online dictionaries, which you can use for free. For example http://dictionary.cambridge.org/dictionary/learner-english/

- to bow
- to shake hands
- to hug / to embrace
- to press palms together
- to rub noses
- to kiss

Reading: activity 1

Scan the following text and match photos 1–6 to the correct country. Can you find a country for each photograph?

New Zealand

Travellers visiting New Zealand are sure to come across the traditional Maori welcoming custom known as the 'hongi'. An ancient tradition, the hongi involves the rubbing or touching of noses when two people meet. It is a symbolic act referred to as the 'ha' or the 'breath of life', which is considered to come directly from the gods.

Tip: Keep your eyes open to avoid misjudging the distance or you could be in for a rather awkward moment, not to mention a very sore nose!

Tibet

It might be bad manners anywhere else in the world, but in Tibet sticking out your tongue is the customary way to welcome people. The tradition dates back to the 9th century during the time of a vicious Tibetan king known as Lang Darma, who had a black tongue. The Tibetan people feared that Lang Darma would be reincarnated so they began greeting each other by sticking out their tongue to prove that they weren't evil. The tradition continues today and is often accompanied by the person placing their palms down in front of their chest.

Tip: Refrain from greeting Tibetans in the traditional way if you have been chewing liquorice.

Mongolia

When welcoming an unfamiliar guest into their home, a Mongol will present the guest with a 'hada' – a strip of silk or cotton. If you are lucky enough to be presented with a hada, you should grasp it gently in both hands while bowing slightly. The giving or receiving of hada, as well as the act of bowing to each other, is a sign of mutual respect, something that is very important in Mongolian culture.

Tip: Depending on what region of Mongolia you visit, the trading of pipes for smoking and the exchange of snuffboxes is also quite common.

Japan

The usual welcome in Japan is a bow, which can range from a small nod of the head to a long, complete ninety degree bend at the waist. If the welcoming takes place on a tatami floor – a traditional type of Japanese flooring – people are required to get on their knees in order to bow. The longer and deeper the bow, the more respect you are showing. Small head bows are common among younger people in Japan as a more casual and informal welcome.

Tip: Most Japanese people do not expect foreigners to know the correct bowing rules so a slight nod of the head is acceptable.

Kenya

Travellers lucky enough to witness the unique customs and traditions of the most well-known tribe in Kenya, the Maasai, will enjoy their vibrant welcoming dance. The Maasai dance is called 'adamu', the jumping dance, and is performed by the warriors of the tribe. Traditionally, the dance begins by the telling of a story and concludes with dancers forming a circle and competing to jump the highest, demonstrating to visitors the strength and bravery of the tribe.

Tip: Be prepared – a drink of a blend of cow's milk and blood is often offered to visitors as part of the traditional welcome.

China

The traditional greeting in China is referred to as the 'kowtow', a custom which involves folding hands, bowing and, if you are female, making a 'wanfu', which involves the folding and moving of hands down by the side of the body. The kowtow can be traced back to the reign of the legendary Emperor Xuan

Yuan, better known as the Yellow Emperor, whose reign began in 2697 BCE.

Tip: Although the kowtow custom is not commonly practised these days, folding of the hands is still widely used and respected.

Thailand

The Thai greeting referred to as the 'wai' is a graceful tradition which requires a person to take a slight bow of the body and head with palms pressed together in a prayer-like fashion and say 'Sawaddee'. Travellers visiting Thailand will notice that hand positions can change: the higher the hands in relation to the face, the more respect the giver of the wai is showing. This custom was originally used to indicate the absence of weapons and is considered to be the ultimate show of respect. It is still used extensively throughout Thailand today.

Tip: Performing the wai might feel strange at first, but you'll soon start to embrace the tradition and come to enjoy greeting people in the traditional Thai way.

www.news.com.au/travel/news/worlds-weirdest-welcomings/story-e6frfq80-1226005607767

❝ Vocabulary 2

Look at the two groups of words. Work in two groups, A and B, and find the words in the text in activity 1. Can you guess the meaning? When you have finished, look up the words in an English dictionary to check if you were correct.

Group A
- to misjudge
- awkward
- bad manners
- to stick your tongue out

Group A
- to refrain from
- to grasp
- a pipe and snuffboxes
- to nod

Now work with students from the other group and tell each other what your words mean.

Reading: activity 2
Read the text again and answer the following questions.

1 What could happen if you keep your eyes closed when greeting people in New Zealand? Give **two** details.

2 Why did the greeting tradition in Tibet start?

3 Apart from receiving 'hada' in Mongolia, what other exchanges can take place? Give **two** details.

4 Who would use a nod as a form of greeting in Japan?

5 Why do the Maasai men jump at the end of their traditional dance? Give **two** reasons.

6 Where and when did the 'kowtow' start?

7 Why did people first adopt the traditional greeting in Thailand? Give **two** details.

Study tip: reading speed

When you have to read quickly, it is a good idea to use headings in the text to locate the correct information. Also, use the scanning reading technique to find the necessary information quickly.

 **Speaking**

Work in small groups and discuss the following.

- How do you greet people in your country?
- Do you greet different types of people in different ways? For example, how do you greet an older person, a friend, someone you don't know very well or someone you meet for the first time?
- Have you ever been to a country where people greeted each other differently? Give details.

Project

Now work in groups. You are going to do some research into how people from around the world greet each other. Try to think of different cultures or tribes that are not particularly well known.

Use the Internet to help you with the research. Read about the common greetings, prepare a wall poster and then give a short presentation to the other groups.

Speaking

Speaking: activity 1

Have you ever taken a speaking exam? Work in small groups and answer the following questions about a speaking paper. Who got most of the answers correct?

> ## Quiz
>
> 1   Do you do the speaking in pairs?
>
> 2   How many parts are there in the speaking exam? How long is each part?
>
> 3   What happens in each part?
>
> 4   Which part are you marked on?
>
> 5   What do you talk about in the warm-up?
>
> 6   Are you allowed to make notes to use in the last part?
>
> 7   How much time do you have to prepare yourself for the last part?
>
> 8   Can you ask the teacher any questions when you are preparing what to say?
>
> 9   Can you deliver a speech in the last part?
>
> 10 Is it a good idea to give short answers? Why? Why not?
>
> 11 Do you only talk about the ideas printed on the card that your teacher will give you?
>
> 12 Can the teacher help you to develop your ideas?

Speaking: activity 2

Look at the sample speaking topic card. The topic is 'Good manners'. Read through the prompts and think what you could talk about. Compare your ideas with other students.

Good manners

It is often said that good manners are disappearing these days, especially amongst young people.

Discuss the topic with the teacher.

Use the following prompts, in the order given below, to develop the conversation.

- The last time you helped somebody.

- In your culture, what you should do when you visit somebody's house for the first time.

- The suggestion that a person with bad manners is a bad person.

- Whether you believe that teaching children good manners these days is more difficult than in the past.

- The view that the fast pace of modern life has made us more selfish.

You may introduce **related** ideas of your own to expand on these prompts.

Remember, you are not allowed to make any written notes.

Study tip: developing your ideas in a conversation

When having a conversation, you should develop your ideas. You can do this by:

- giving examples of what you have said
- talking about personal experience
- giving your opinion on the topic
- justifying your opinion
- making comparisons (e.g. now and the past, your generation and your parents' generation, your country with another country)
- discussing the advantages and disadvantages.

Speaking: activity 3

Listen (track 2) to two students answering the first prompt, 'the last time you helped somebody'. Who gave the better answer and why?

Did the students expand their answers? If so, how did they do it?

Speaking: activity 4

Work in pairs and look at Recording 1 in Transcript 1. How could you expand the student's answers? Act out the conversation between the student and the teacher.

Speaking: activity 5

Work in pairs again. Imagine you are taking a speaking exam yourself. Use the topic card 'Good manners'. Decide who the student is and who the teacher is. Have a conversation together. You can use the ideas you thought of in activity 2.

Teacher: ask the student extra questions about what they have said.

Student: try to develop your ideas by expanding your answers.

See Transcript 1 at the back of the book.

🔊 Listening

Pre-listening activity

You are going to listen to students who are studying in the United Kingdom. They are talking about their experiences. Work in small groups and discuss what you would miss from your country if you studied abroad. Say why you would miss these things. Then compare your answers with the other groups. What is the most common thing people would miss and why?

Listening: activity 1

Before you listen to the recordings, look at the following statements about this type of listening exercise. Work in pairs and decide whether these statements are **true** or **false**. Then read the instructions carefully and check if you were correct.

Statements

1   It is a good idea to read the questions as you listen to the recordings.

2   There are six recordings to listen to.

3   There are two questions for each recording.

4   You can write as many words in the answer as you want. The important thing is that you include the correct answer.

5   You will hear the recordings twice.

6   If you answer all the questions during the first listening, you do not have to pay attention when the recordings are played the second time.

Instructions

> In this type of listening exercise you will listen to four short recordings. These could be short conversations, announcements, telephone messages etc. Before you listen, make sure you read the questions very carefully and circle, or underline, the key words. These key words are often the question words (e.g. *what, where, why,* etc.). For each recording, there are two questions to answer. Check if you need to listen for one, or two details for each question. You only need to write up to three words for each question, no more. You will hear each recording twice.
>
> Try to get all answers the first time you listen so that you can use the second listening to check your answers.

Listening: activity 2

Before you listen to the four students talking about their experiences abroad, read these questions and underline the key words.

1   a   What **two** things from her country does the student miss the most?

....

....

b What food from the UK does she like?

....

....

2 a How did the student feel after he started his course?

....

....

b Where does the student study after school?

....

....

3 a What did the student drink at her friend's house?

....

....

b What do people put in the drink in the student's home country?
Give **two** details.

....

....

4 a Who does the student call most using Skype?

....

....

b When does he usually use Skype?

....

....

Did you know?

Skype was first released in 2003 and it was developed in Estonia by two engineers, Niklas Zennstrom and Janus Friis.

Listening: activity 3

You are now going to listen to the interviews in track 3 with four students who are studying English in the UK. They are talking about their first experiences after their arrival in the country. Listen to the interviews and answer the questions in activity 2.

See Transcript 2 at the back of the book.

Project

If there is someone at your school who comes from a different country or region, prepare a short interview with them about their social conventions. Think about different situations (e.g. greetings, table manners, dress code, visiting somebody for the first time, etc.) and appropriate questions. Then you can compare your findings with the conventions in your country or region and have a class discussion about this.

Imagine you have just spent a holiday with your friend's family who come from a different country to you. They made you feel very welcome and you have decided to write a thank you letter to them.

In your letter:

- thank them for their generosity
- say what you particularly enjoyed about your visit
- say what you have learnt from your visit
- invite them to stay with your family.

✏ Writing 1

Writing: activity 1

Look at this letter you have received from your pen pal. Skim read it and say why it was written.

Hi Fatma,

Hope you're doing OK. Sorry I haven't been in touch for a while, but I've been really busy with my course. The end of term tests are coming up so there's a lot of revision to do.

Now, guess what! I've got some really exciting news for you. I'm coming to your country for a couple of weeks. My mum finally agreed to let me go on my own to visit my cousin in the capital. I'm going to stay with his family, but it would be really cool if we could meet up as well. Let me know what you think and if you fancy doing anything together. If it's not too much bother, I'd really love to see some of the sights you were telling me about. Is that possible?

Also, I was going to ask you a favour. I don't want to get into any embarrassing situations like when I'm meeting people for the first time or when I go and visit somebody's house and have dinner with them. Do you think you could drop me a line and give me some tips about what to do and what to watch out for? That'd be really helpful.

Anyway, must rush now. My history lesson starts in a couple of minutes. Will tweet you soon to let you know how my exams went. Oh, by the way, you want to check out Julie's photos from her trip to Malaysia on her Facebook page. They're awesome.

Hope to see you soon.

Lots of love,

Monica

> **Key term: phrasal verbs and idioms**
>
> Phrasal verbs and idioms are phrases used in informal English when we talk or write to somebody we know.
>
> For example:
> 1 *I need to* **look up** *the meaning. I don't understand it.* 'Look up' is a phrasal verb that means **to find information about something.**
> 2 *Helena's got* **green fingers**. This is an idiom that means Helena's **good at gardening**.

Writing: activity 2

Analysing a piece of writing

Below are some points you should consider before writing an informal letter/email. Look at Monica's letter and answer the questions.

1 Who is this letter for?

2 Is the letter formal or informal?

3 How many paragraphs are there?

4 What information did Monica put in each paragraph?

5 What is the opening greeting?

6 What is the greeting at the end of the letter?

7 Can you leave words out and use note-like sentences? Find one example.

8 Can you use short forms? Find a few examples.

9 Can you use phrasal verbs and idioms? Are there any examples in the text?

🍎 Vocabulary 3

Now look at Monica's letter again in activity 1 and find the words/phrases that mean the same as the following:

1 be in contact with somebody

2 You'll never believe this, but … (to introduce surprising news)

3 two or three

4 would like to / feel like something

5 if you don't mind …

6 interesting or important buildings and places in a city

7 I'd like to ask you for help

8 write to me

9 to be careful about something

10 to have a look at something

Writing: activity 3

Planning a piece of writing

You are going to write back to Monica and answer her questions. Consider the following:

- What are the main points you should mention in your letter?
- How many paragraphs are you going to use?
- What information will you include in each paragraph?
- How will you start your letter?
- How will you finish your letter?

⊕ Language focus

Giving advice and making suggestions

Analysis

Monica asked you to give her some useful tips in your reply. When you give tips to somebody, you give them advice or make suggestions. Look at the sentences below and tick those that can be used to give advice to people, or make suggestions. There are two sentences that are not used for advice or suggestions.

1   You should wear something smart.

2   How about going to the movies tonight?

3   If I were you, I'd buy something small, like flowers or chocolates.

4   You'd better take your shoes off.

5   Why don't you buy her a cake?

6   Always remember to shake hands with people.

7   I reckon it's going to be a great trip.

8   Resist the temptation to speak during meal times.

9   Avoid talking too loudly on your mobile phone on public transport.

10 It's a good idea to pay a compliment to the host about their house.

11 I was wondering if you could come round a bit earlier today.

Verb forms

Now work in pairs. Look at the sentences 1–11 again and find the verb forms. Do we need the infinitive ('to do'), the bare infinitive ('do') or the -ing form ('doing') after the first verb, the preposition, or the phrase? Discuss the verb forms in each of the sentences with your partner.

For example: *You **should wear** something smart.*
'Should' is followed by a bare infinitive verb form.

Practice

Exercise 1

Read these answers given by some students. Are they correct? What mistakes can you find? Think about grammar, missing words, spelling and punctuation. Work with your partner and try to correct them.

1   You should to take your shoes of. (2 mistakes)

2   Before going abroad you'd better reserch some comon social conventions. (3 mistakes)

3   Allways remember watching your personal belonggings. (3 mistakes)

4   When you visit london, its a good idea to queu for the bus. (3 mistakes)

5   Avoid to eat food with ur hands. (2 mistakes)

6   Resist temtation to answer the phone when your in the cinema. (3 mistakes)

Exercise 2

Look at these photographs. What problems could these people have? What advice would you give them to avoid these problems?

Activate your English

Think of a few problems you have had – these problems can be real or you can make them up. For example, problems you had when you travelled to a foreign country, when you joined this school, problems with your studies or friends, everyday problems, etc.

One student will then explain their problems and the other student will give advice. Before you start, make rough notes. Then work in pairs and make a dialogue. Try to use the useful phrases from this Language focus section.

When you have finished your dialogue, swap roles with the other student and do the role-play again.

 # Writing 2

Writing: activity 1

Writing correction code

Look at the symbols and the examples, which contain mistakes. Can you guess the meaning of each symbol?

Symbol	Meaning	Example
Sp		I recieved your letter yesterday.
WO		I've been never to Japan.
T		I never went to New York before.
WF		You look beautifully.
Gr		He like to 'google' informations.
∧		She said goodbye me and got on train.
/		It was too very difficult.
( )		He repeated again his answer.
?		I how him clean in kitchen with me.
WW		I make my homework every day.
R		I'm going to get some bread. Moreover, I'm getting my hair done.
P		whats your name. im called maria. my brother live's in the uk.
//		... and waving goodbye, she left for California. Many years later, John had a job offer ...
✓		I love coming here because I'm really learning a lot and I've made so many friends.

Study tip:
Correcting written work

If you want to improve your writing, remember to do two things.

1 Proofread your written work after you have finished writing it.

2 We learn from our own mistakes! This means when your teacher gives your written work back to you, it is a good idea to write the same piece again, but without the mistakes. This makes you more aware of what you do wrong and, hopefully, you won't make the same mistakes again.

Key term: proofreading

Proofreading is a type of reading that focuses on finding mistakes in a text.

Writing: activity 2

Read the following email, which was written as an answer to the letter in Writing 1: activity 1. The student has made several mistakes. They have been underlined for you. Decide what type of mistakes they are and then correct them.

13

New Message

To: ☐   From: ☐

Hi Monica,

It was <u>grate</u> to hear from you. Hope your exams went OK and you passed with flying colours. I'm so excited that you <u>come</u> and can't wait to meet up with you. How could you think that <u>Id</u> miss the opportunity to see you?

Anyway, let me tell you what sightseeing we can do together in Prague. I know your time in Prague will be limited because you're going to spend most of the time <u>for</u> your family, but you definitely must see the historical city centre. It's simply stunning; you've got to see it for yourself. It is <u>quiet</u> small so you can walk everywhere. I think we should walk from Wenceslas <u>square</u> to Prague Castle and just admire all the beautiful architecture. When you get <u>tired we</u> can always stop in one of the many cafés that <u>is</u> scattered along the way and have a cup of coffee. <u>what</u> do you <u>reckon.</u> Let me know what you think.

As for your question about visiting somebody's house, there are <u>sure</u> things you have to <u>bare</u> in mind. First of all, remember to take your shoes off. It is very rude if you don't. Also, if I <u>was</u> you, I'd get some flowers or <u>box</u> of chocolates to give to your cousin's family. It's polite to bring a small present when you're visiting somebody for the first time. During <u>diner</u> you really have to follow a few rules. Even if <u>your</u> very hungry, resist the temptation to start <u>eat</u> before everybody else is ready to start. Also, remember to say, 'Enjoy your meal' before you start. We don't tend to speak during meal times and be careful <u>to not</u> slurp! It is really rude if you do. I think that's it really. If you have any more <u>questions just</u> text me and <u>I be</u> more than happy to help.

Had a look at Julie's photos. They're great. Wish I could go there. Maybe one day.

Take care and see you soon.

Love,

Fatma

Writing: activity 3

Now look back at your own written work that the teacher has corrected and rewrite it without the mistakes.

Summary

Can you remember …

- **four** different types of greetings?
- the traditional greeting in China?
- which parts of the body you use when you 'nod' and 'shake'?
- how many parts there are in your speaking paper and which one is assessed?
- what you should do before you listen to the recordings in your listening paper?
- what skimming is? Do you read for detail or for gist?
- if you can leave words out in an informal letter/email?
- what information you can put in the opening and closing paragraphs in an informal letter/email?

- the phrase that means 'two or three'?
- **three** phrases to give advice?
- what verb form you need in the following phrases? 'If I were you, I'd …'; 'It's a good idea …'; 'How about …?'
- what the following correction code symbols mean? Sp; T; WF
- what the correction code symbol is for a missing word and for a new paragraph?
- what the mistakes are in the following sentence and what symbols your teacher would use? 'I never have gone in chile, but I want go soon there.'

Progress check

Go back to the Objectives at the beginning of this chapter and assess your progress. Use the symbols below to show how confident you feel about your learning progress.

I am very good at this.	✓ ✓
I am OK, but I need a bit more practice.	✓
I can't do this yet and I need to look at this section again.	✗

Chapter 2:
Celebrations round the world

Objectives

In this chapter, you will learn and practise:

- reading skills – answering questions about festivals
- speaking skills – discussing the topic of festivals and celebrations
- listening skills – completing sentences about a carnival
- writing skills – writing a letter to a friend about a celebration.

You will also learn and practise the following **language skills:**

- the passive voice
- phrasal verbs and fixed expressions
- linkers.

You will 'Activate your English' by:

- giving a formal talk on a range of topics
- using phrasal verbs in discussions.

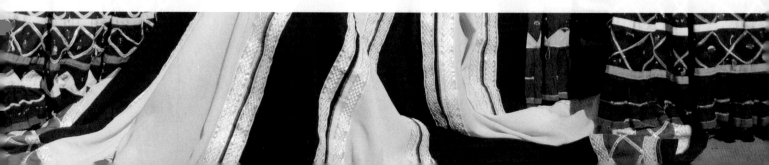

Chapter 2: Celebrations round the world

📖 Reading

Festival of Colours

Radish Festival

Songkran Water Festival

Boryeong Mud Festival

Pre-reading activity

Look at the photographs. Do you know any of the festivals? Can you guess from the photographs what happens during each festival?

Reading: activity 1

Work in four groups. Each group is going to read about one of the festivals. Make a copy of the following table. Scan the text that talks about your festival and find the information needed to complete the table. When you have finished, tell the other students about your festival. Use the information from the table as your notes.

When you listen to the other groups talking about their festivals, fill in the missing information for the three remaining festivals.

Festival	Where	When	Why	What happens
Festival of Colours				
Radish Festival				
Songkran Water Festival				
Boryeong Mud Festival				

Did you know?

The colour red is typical for a wedding in India.

While the colour white is often worn by brides in weddings in the western countries, in India this colour represents mourning after somebody has died.

Did you know?

Bangkok, the capital of Thailand, has the highest average temperature of any city in the world. The average temperature stays above 30 °C throughout the year.

Festival of Colours

This Hindu festival is celebrated in India and is also known as 'Holi'. It is held in springtime and is associated with Krishna, one of the most popular gods in the Hindu religion. This festival celebrates the victory of good over evil and it also welcomes the arrival of spring. In most festivals people tend to put on their best clothes, but not for this one – quite the opposite, in fact. In preparation for the celebration, people rummage through their wardrobes and dig out some old clothes to wear. This is because during this celebration powder paints, also known as 'gulal', are thrown at your relatives, friends, neighbours and even strangers. In some parts of India they also use wet paints.

Radish Festival

This Mexican festival is also known as 'Noche de Rabanos'. It is held in a town called Oaxaca every year on 23rd December. People use radishes, which are the symbol of Christmas in Mexico, to carve out small sculptures. These sculptures are used to greet the coming Christmas Day. The main event takes place in the central square of Oaxaca and anyone can join the competition. The winner's picture is then printed in the local newspaper. The winning sculptures have an amazing amount of intricate detail and can weigh up to three kilograms. The carving starts a week before the festival and all the radishes are kept fresh by being sprayed with water.

www.festivalpig.com/Oaxaca-Radish-Festival.html

Songkran Water Festival

This festival is held in mid-April to celebrate the traditional New Year in Thailand. Nobody is safe from what is probably the largest 'water fight' in the world which can go on for three days. This festival is all about purifying yourself and making a fresh start in the New Year. Even though this festival has religious roots, over the years it is the water fights that have been drawing the crowds. Another benefit to getting drenched is the welcome relief from the sometimes unbearable heat, which can reach almost 40 °C. However, it is not only the water throwing that makes it fun, it is also all the music and dancing that goes on in the streets.

Boryeong Mud Festival

Every year between 14th and 24th July something very unusual happens in the town of Boryeong in South Korea – the Mud Festival. The local soil is said to be rich in minerals, which are supposed to have a beneficial effect on your skin. A lot of trucks are needed to collect enough mud from around the town and transport it to Daecheon Beach just outside Boryeong for the festival. This celebration draws not only the locals, but also around two million visitors from outside the city and further afield. Competitions, such as mud wrestling, mud skiing and even mud swimming, are all part of the fun to be found at the festival.

Key term: context

This is the general situation in which something happens and this situation helps to explain it.

In a text it is all the surrounding words that help you understand the situation or meaning.

Study tip:
Guessing vocabulary from the context

When your reading is being tested, you usually cannot use a dictionary. That is why it is important to train your brain to guess the meaning from the context.

All these things can help you.

- Look at the sentences before and after the unknown word.
- Think – is there a prefix like 'dis-' to signal a negative meaning?
- Are there any examples given after the word to help you guess?
- Is the word a noun, an adjective or a verb?

 # Vocabulary 1

Work in the same four groups. Look at the highlighted words in the text you have just read. Try to guess the meaning of these words from the **context** and then check your ideas with the other students in your group. Only check in an English dictionary if you are not sure about the meaning.

Tell the students in the other groups what the words in your text mean.

Reading: activity 2
Now read all four texts and answer the following questions.

1   What sort of clothes do people wear during the Festival of Colours?
2   In the Radish Festival, why were radishes chosen for the carving?
3   Why are the winning sculptures special? Give **two** examples.
4   How do contestants make sure that the radishes stay looking good for 23rd December?
5   Apart from being good fun and drawing the crowds, is there another reason why you might enjoy getting wet during the Water Festival?
6   Where does the mud come from and how does it get to the location where the Mud Festival takes place?
7   Who attends the Mud Festival?

Speaking

Work in groups and answer the questions below. Do not forget to expand your answers.

1   Would you like to take part in any of the four festivals? Why? Why not?
2   Do you have any similar festivals in your country?
3   What do you do in your country to welcome the New Year?
4   Do you have any festivals to welcome a different season?
5   Are there any festivals in your country that involve water?
6   Are there any festivals in your country that require the use of certain foods?

 Study tip:
Expanding answers
Remember to expand your answers. If the question requires a yes/no answer, this is not enough. Always give examples, compare what used to happen and what happens now, or give some personal experience.

Project

There are a lot of festivals around the world. Choose a festival that you find interesting or unusual and prepare a short talk. You can use the Internet or encyclopaedias to find information you need.

Remember it is always more interesting for the audience if you use some photos, graphs, diagrams, etc. to go with your talk. You will also keep people interested if you include some surprising, shocking or humorous facts.

At the end of your talk, don't forget to ask your classmates if they have any questions about the festival you have talked about.

Useful language expressions

- It is held .... to celebrate ....
- People tend to ....
- You can see people .... (+ -*ing*)
- There are a lot of people ....(+ -*ing*)
- I've never seen anything like it before in my life.

Imagine you have just come back from a holiday. While you were there, you attended a local festival. You thought it was a very good festival and people should know about it.

You have decided to write an online review using some of the information from your talk. Don't forget to say what you enjoyed most about the festival and why people should see it too.

 # Language focus

The passive voice

Analysis

Look at these sentences taken from the Reading section.

A This Hindu festival is celebrated in India.

B Powder paints are thrown at your relatives, friends, neighbours and even strangers.

C It is held in a town called Oaxaca.

D This Mexican festival is also known as 'Noche de Rabanos'.

Now answer the questions below:

1 What are the two verbs that are used in each sentence?

2 Now change the four sentences into the past simple tense. Which verb changes when we want to change the tense in the passive voice?

3 Why do you use the passive voice? Are you interested in who does the action or what happens?

4 Is the passive voice used more commonly in formal or informal situations?

Tenses

Look at these passive sentences in different tenses. Highlight the tense in each sentence. What tense is it? Choose from the five options given. How does the verb 'to be' change in each tense?

> **Key term: past participle verb forms**
>
> These are verb forms that are used, for example, in the passive voice. For regular verbs, you only need to add -*ed* to the verb (e.g. **cook – cooked**). For irregular verbs, the past participle forms vary (e.g. **buy – bought, write – written, do – done**).

1   A letter was sent out to all students on Monday.

2   In future most traditions will be lost.

3   All questions are going to be answered by the Head teacher.

4   All the tickets for the festival have been sold.

5   The photographs were taken by our students last year.

6   I'm always told to be more careful.

7   We've been invited to the Summer Festival by our friend.

| future 'going to' |
| future 'will' |
| present simple |
| present perfect |
| past simple |

Pronunciation

Listen to the following sentences in track 4 and focus on the underlined auxiliary verbs. How do we pronounce them?

Is the pronunciation of the auxiliary verbs strong or weak? Choose the correct answer below.

Weak sounds appear in:

*   short answers
*   full sentences.

Now listen again and copy the pronunciation.

1   It <u>has</u> <u>been</u> repaired.

2   It <u>was</u> made very popular in the sixties.

3   They <u>were</u> carved out of radishes.

4   It <u>can</u> be used as a decoration.

5   Yes, it <u>has</u>.

6   Yes, it <u>was</u>.

7   Yes, they <u>were</u>.

8   Yes, it <u>can</u>.

See Transcript 3 at the back of the book.

Practice

Exercise 1

Complete the gaps with the passive voice in the correct tense.

1   Every time I decide to go to a party I end up staying at home because it .... (cancel).

2   The school assembly .... (hold) in the gym tomorrow morning at 9 o'clock.

3   My city .... actually .... (build) by the Romans many centuries ago.

4   I'm so happy at the moment. I .... just .... (give) some very good news about my exam by the Head teacher.

5   I decided to ask my father if I could have my room redecorated and he said 'yes'! It .... (do) very soon, but we haven't decided when exactly yet.

21

6   My homework .... (check) by my brother who's excellent at English so I hope I can get a good mark for this one.

7   These celebratory cakes .... (make) with dried fruits and nuts.

8   Tests .... (take) by all classes to check their progress.

9   You just have to wait and see. It .... all .... (reveal) next week. Then you can hear the name of the winners announced during a special ceremony.

10   The celebration .... (spoil) by the awful weather. We had to cancel all the outdoor activities and only keep the indoor dance competition.

11   Don't worry, everything is under control. The flowers and decorations .... (order). All your friends .... (inform) about the time of your birthday party.

Exercise 2
Practise using the passive voice in sentences. For each situation, think what tense would be the most appropriate and then try to **write three to five sentences**.

Think of one activity that you do every day (e.g. make tea). What is done?

For example:

•   First, the kettle is filled with water.

Now think what preparation had to be done before your last birthday party or any other celebration you went to.

For example:

•   First, my friends were invited.

Think of the place/city where you live. What has changed?

For example:

•   A new bridge has been built across the river.

What will be done at the end of this academic year?

For example:

•   Students will be given their final reports.

Activate your English
Work in small groups. Each of you is going to give a short talk about one of the topics below. Choose one and prepare notes for your talk. Remember to use the passive voice to make your talk sound more formal. Then, give your talk to the other students in your group.

A popular festival in your country.	Describe preparations for your last trip.	How to prepare your favourite dish.
Recent news you have heard or read.	What life will be like in the future.	Recent changes at your school.

🔊 Listening

Listening: activity 1
Listen to an interview with Dana in track 5. What kind of celebration is she talking about? Did she enjoy it? Why? Why not? (Give examples.)

Listening: activity 2
Now look at the form. Focus on the gaps and try to predict what type of information is missing.

Then listen to the recording and fill in the gaps. Write one or two words only in each gap. You will hear the recording twice.

The Carnival in Rio

A Dana's mum and dad went to live in Portugal because of ....

B Dana didn't want to study .... like her father.

C During Dana's studies some .... gave her jobs helping with dance performances.

D Dana went to Brazil in .... for the first time.

E Occasionally people continue with the Carnival for nearly ....

F Apart from being the largest carnival, people think it's also the .... one.

G The judges award points for the .... from people watching the parade, among other things.

H It is said that the carnival was introduced to Brazil by ....

See Transcript 4 at the back of the book.

🔊 Vocabulary 2

Phrasal verbs and fixed expressions
Read Transcript 4 from the previous listening activity. Work in two groups and look through the text. One group should look for examples of **phrasal verbs** and the other group for other **fixed expressions**. When you find some, write them down and share them with the other group. Don't worry about their meaning at this point.

🔑 Key term: phrasal verbs

Phrasal verbs are verbs with one or two particles (e.g. *up, off, over, to*, etc.) and can change their meaning compared with standard verbs.

For example: *The plane takes off at 4.55 in the afternoon.* The phrasal verb **to take off** in this sentence doesn't mean to 'take something off'. It means when a plane **leaves the ground.**

23

Key term: fixed expressions

In English you often come across **fixed expressions**. These are words that often appear together and, like **phrasal verbs**, change their meaning.

Sometimes there are two words together (e.g. *to do homework, to make a mistake*). These are called **collocations**. Sometimes there are three or more words (e.g. *to be in charge of something*).

If you use these expressions, you will sound more natural, just like a native speaker.

Study tip: Dictionary work

When looking up phrasal verbs in a dictionary, look up the standard verb (e.g. *take*) and then look for the correct particle (e.g. *up, over, off*). Particles are listed in alphabetical order. This means that 'take after' would appear before 'take on', etc.

Did you know?

- All major bridges leading to and from Manhattan were designed by Swiss engineers.
- The only Olympic Games museum in the world is in Lausanne, Switzerland.
- The trains in Switzerland are on time 97 per cent of the time.

Exercise 1

Can you match the following definitions to the words you found in the transcript? They appear in the same order as in the transcript.

1 the process when a child becomes an adult (phrasal verb)
2 to experience something yourself, not just read about it (fixed expression)
3 really amazing (fixed expression)
4 to continue (phrasal verb)
5 to decide on something after discussing it (phrasal verb)
6 to do something repeatedly (fixed expressions)
7 to learn new information (phrasal verb)

Activate your English

Work in groups of three and discuss the following:

1 If you had the choice, where would you like to grow up?
2 What is difficult about growing up?
3 Where do you find out about the latest news in music or fashion? Why do you prefer this source of news?
4 What would you like to experience or see first-hand? Why?
5 Is there anything you had to do over and over again as a child that you really hated?
6 Is there an activity that you can carry on doing without getting bored? Why do you love it so much?

 # Writing

Writing: activity 1

Read the following letter and answer the questions. Ignore the numbers in the letter for this activity – they are used in activity 2.

1 Who wrote the letter?
2 Do Aisha and Mariana know each other? Are they friends?
3 What are the two main events described in the letter?
4 What is the purpose of the last paragraph?

24

New Message

To : _____   From: _____

Hello Aisha,

Sorry I've been neglecting you a bit ....(1) I've been away for my winter break. Hope your break was OK ....
(2) you managed to get some rest.

................(3), I'm writing this email ....(4) I want to tell you about my break. ....(5)!
I went to Switzerland. I'm sure you remember ....(6). I always wanted to go there ....(7) I was a child.
I can't remember ....(8) I told you – one of my best friends, Mariana, lives there. She lives in the French canton
called 'Vaud'. I went there for two weeks. The first week we stayed with her family near Lausanne. ....(9), for the
second week, she took me to the mountains. We saw one of the highest mountains in Switzerland called the 'Matterhorn'. We
................(10) went skiing ....(11) it was the first time for me, it went a bit wrong. ....(12),
I had a little accident. I fell over, broke my expensive skis ....(13) bumped my head very hard. For the rest of the
week, I just watched my friends having fun in the snow .... (14) I was sipping tea on the veranda of our chalet.
....................................(15), a chalet is a type of mountain cottage in Switzerland.

....(16) I want to tell you about is our special evening eating 'fondue'. It's a kind of a tradition. A lot
of people in Switzerland eat this dish in wintertime mostly ....(17) it's quite heavy for hot weather. Each region has its own
variation of this cheese dish. I loved it ....(18) a lot of people get together ....(19) it's also a social
get-together, not just food. You melt the cheese in a special pot ....(20) put a piece of bread on a special
long fork ....(21) you dip in the melted cheese. It's delish! You know I'm a cheese lover ....(22) it was like
cheese heaven for me. It was a great evening for making new friends too. You eat a bit, chat, eat a bit and chat again. I had a
really good time with Mariana. ....(23) it was hard to leave at the end of my stay.

....(24), I invited Mariana to come and stay with us next month. Do you fancy coming too? It would be
really cool. We could all spend some time together ....(25) you could get to know Mariana a bit more. She's such a
good laugh. Please say yes! ....(26), if you can't, there's always next year.

Can't wait to hear from you. Give my love to your parents and little brother.

Lots of love,

Claire

Writing: activity 2

Look at the letter in activity 1 again. Are the sentences **complex** or not? Why?

Try to complete the gaps with the most suitable **linker**. Choose from the
selection below. Remember – some linkers are used more than once.

> **Key term: clauses**
>
> Clauses are parts of a sentence.
> They consist of a subject and a
> verb. A sentence can have more
> than one clause.
>
> For example: **It's raining today**,
> *but* **I don't mind**. This sentence
> has two clauses.

so	and	that reminds me
then	because	but	guess what
and as	unfortunately	since	however
anyway	that's why	if	another thing
which	also	while	and then
that	by the way		

Key term: complex sentences

Complex sentences have more than one clause.

For example: *I had a cheese sandwich*, which *I didn't like very much*, and then *I bought some ice-cream*. This sentence is complex and has three clauses.

These clauses are joined together with 'which' and 'and then'. 'which' gives us more detail about the sandwich. 'and then' adds new information.

Study tip:
Complex sentences in speaking and writing
It is a good idea to use complex sentences in your speaking and writing. They will make your performance sound more natural.

Key term: linkers

Linkers are like 'glue' in the text. Without them, texts sound broken and unnatural.

Linkers are words or phrases that link sentences together which make the sentence more complex, but more natural-sounding. We also use linkers to start paragraphs or to link ideas together.

Study tip:
Linkers in emails to a friend
If you use linkers, this will improve the quality of your writing and make it sound more natural. Just be careful to use the correct linkers. Some of them are too formal and would not be suitable for an informal email (e.g. *furthermore, in addition to that*).

Writing: activity 3

Now look at the following categories. Put the linkers from activity 2 in the correct category. There are some linkers that do not go in any of the categories.

1 Adding more information

2 Two opposing/contrasting ideas together

3 Result

4 Explaining why something happened

5 Time

6 To introduce some bad news

7 Adding extra detail about things

Writing: activity 4

Now look at the following categories. Choose the best linker(s) from activity 2 for each category. These linkers are used when you start a new idea or a new paragraph.

1 You want to change the topic; you start a new idea.

2 You want to say something surprising.

3 You want to add something new, normally something interesting or important that you've just remembered.

Writing: activity 5

Look at the three columns and match the correct parts together. Notice the punctuation used at the end of some of the sentences in the first column. This means that some linkers will need a capital letter and some will not. Which linkers will need a capital letter?

Two of the linkers also need a comma. Can you decide which ones? Now rewrite the sentences in full with the correct punctuation.

1	Yesterday it was raining really hard.	which	A	have you met before?
2	We bought some food, Tiago is bringing some DVDs	by the way	B	we'll definitely make it another time.
3	This is my classmate Yumi.	however	C	the heat was unbearable.
4	I'd love to fly to the Rio Carnival.	but	D	we had to cancel the picnic.
5	We're going to a festival in Thailand	while	E	I can't afford the airfare.
6	We can't come and visit this year	because	F	involves a lot of water throwing.
7	The school football match was cancelled	that's why	G	I was having dinner with my family.
8	My mobile rang	and	H	you can be responsible for preparing the room.

Writing: activity 6

Work in pairs. Cover up the last column in activity 5. Complete each sentence with your own idea. For example: Yesterday it was raining really hard. That's why *I watched TV all day long.*

Now cover up the middle and the last columns. Complete the sentences in the first column with your own ideas. You can use different linkers if you want. Write your ideas on strips of paper. For example: Yesterday it was raining … / … *However, I played football outside the whole afternoon.* When you write your answers on the strip of paper, only include your idea, but not the first sentence.

When you have finished, give your answers to another pair and test them to see if they can match your ideas to the correct first sentence in their books.

Writing: activity 7

Now you are ready to write your own letter to a friend. Imagine you are writing to a friend about a festival, celebration or special event you've been to. In your letter you should mention:

- where it was and why you went there
- what people did
- why you enjoyed it.

In your letter, try to use linkers to improve your writing. Don't forget to look at the sample letter in this section.

Your letter should be between 100 and 150 words long.

Summary

Can you remember …

- **one** interesting fact about each of the unusual festivals?
- where the most famous carnival is?
- what a popular winter dish in Switzerland is?
- the name of a mountain in Switzerland?
- how to make your talk more interesting for the audience?
- what you should do at the end of your talk?
- how to make the passive voice? What two verbs are needed?
- what the past participle forms are for these verbs: *buy, choose, find, sing, teach*?
- if the following sentence is correct? 'The students was tell to bring sandwiches for the picnic.'

- what a phrasal verb is? Can you give three examples?
- what words are missing from the following fixed expressions? 'experience something first ….'; 'do something over and over …'; 'something is ……………………………… this world'
- what complex sentences are? Can you make this sentence complex? 'I went to Shanghai.'
- why we use linkers? how to make sentences with these five linkers: 'however'; 'which'; 'that's why'; 'that reminds me'; 'while'?
- how to use 'furthermore' in a letter to a friend?

Progress check

Go back to the Objectives at the beginning of this chapter and assess your progress. Use the symbols below to show how confident you feel about your learning progress.

I am very good at this. ✓ ✓

I am OK, but I need a bit more practice. ✓

I can't do this yet and I need to look at this section again. ✗

Chapter 3:
The natural environment

Objectives

In this chapter, you will learn and practise:

- reading skills – taking notes about extreme natural places
- speaking skills – discussing personal experiences and feelings
- listening skills – matching speakers to the correct feeling about an experience
- writing skills – writing an article about travelling and getting new experiences; using the correct style; and language.

You will also learn and practise the following language skills:

- vocabulary sets – extreme natural places
- comparative and superlative forms of adjectives.

You will 'Activate your English' by:

- stating opinions about a range of topics, agreeing and disagreeing
- giving a personal account of past experiences.

Chapter 3: **The natural environment**

📖 Reading

Pre-reading activity

Work in small groups and discuss the following points.

Have you ever been to or read about:

- an extremely cold place
- an extremely hot place
- a very densely populated place
- a very isolated place
- very high mountains
- a really wet place?

Tell the others in the group what the place is called, where it is, why it is special or different and how you felt visiting that place. If you have read about the place, tell the other students if you would like to visit it.

Reading: activity 1

You are going to read five short entries from an encyclopaedia about extreme places on Earth. First, check that you understand the words that have been underlined below.

Before you read the entries, work in pairs to see if you know the names of the places in the list below. Try to guess if you don't know. Compare your answers with other pairs.

The places are:

1 the hottest place on Earth

2 the coldest place where people <u>settle down</u> to live

3 the most <u>isolated</u> place <u>inhabited</u> by people

4 the highest point <u>measured</u> from the centre of the Earth

5 the lowest place <u>on land</u>.

Now scan the articles and find the correct answers. How many did you get right?

Nature's records: extreme places on Earth

1 There is considerable interest in finding the hottest spot on Earth. Many people believe it is in Al Azizyah, Libya, where a record temperature of 57.8 °C has been recorded. The second hottest place is thought to be in Death Valley, California, USA, where the temperature got up to 56.6 °C in 1913. According to other sources, a NASA satellite recorded surface temperatures as high as 71 °C in the Lut Desert of Iran, supposedly the hottest temperature ever recorded on the surface of the Earth. This region, which covers an area of about 480 km, is called Gandom Beriyan (the 'toasted wheat').

2 Mount Everest is known as the highest mountain in the world. Climbers from all over the world travel to Everest hoping to earn the distinction of climbing the 'World's Highest'. The peak of Mount Everest is 8848 m above sea level, which makes it the mountain with the highest altitude.

However, not many people are aware of Mount Chimborazo in Ecuador. This mountain has an altitude of 6310 m, which is less than Mount Everest. Chimborazo on the other hand has the distinction of being the highest mountain above the centre of the Earth. This is because the Earth is not a perfect sphere and it is wider towards the equator. Chimborazo is just one degree south of the equator and it is 6384 km from the centre of the Earth, which is about 2 km more than Mount Everest. The Ecuadorians are proud of this interesting fact. Nonetheless, Chimborazo cannot compare in difficulty, lack of oxygen, nor in fame, to Mount Everest.

3 The most isolated inhabited island group in the world, Tristan de Cunha in the southern Atlantic Ocean, is so tiny that its main island has no runway for planes to land on. It is home to 272 people who share just eight surnames. Some inhabitants suffer from hereditary complaints like asthma and glaucoma. This group of islands was made part of the United Kingdom in the 1800s – the island's inhabitants have a British postal code. Although they can order things online, it takes a very long time for their orders to arrive. That is one disadvantage of living on a group of islands 3218 km away from the nearest continent.

4 Oymyakon is a village in the Sakha Republic in Russia and is located along the Indigirka River. The population of the village is 800 and on 26th January 1926, a temperature of −71.2 °C was recorded there. This is the lowest recorded temperature for any permanently inhabited location on Earth. It is also the lowest temperature recorded in the Northern Hemisphere. The lowest temperature ever recorded on Earth was −93.2 °C in Antarctica on 10th August, 2010.

5 The Dead Sea, on the border of Jordan and Israel, is the lowest point on dry land on the Earth's surface. Its surface and shores are 422 m below sea level. The road around the Dead Sea is also

the lowest road on Earth. It is famous for its salinity which is over ten times higher than the salinity of the Mediterranean Sea. The Dead Sea is also said to be home of the first health retreat. Due to the extreme salt content, no life can survive in the sea. That is why it is called the Dead Sea.

www.oddee.com/item_96770.aspx

Did you know?

- The Dead Sea is, in fact, a lake.
- The Dead Sea minerals help skin tissue to heal and make your bones and teeth stronger. The water also acts as a disinfectant.

Study tip: Locating information in text

When you are answering reading questions, check if you are given a time limit.

You need to locate the required information quickly in each text. Here are some tips to help you speed up your reading.

1 Look at the headings and sub-headings in the text to help you locate information (e.g. in leaflets or articles).
2 If you need to look for facts, look for numbers in the text (e.g. years, weight, temperature, etc.)
3 Are there any names or specific words in the question that are likely to be repeated in the text (e.g. *the Dead Sea, hemisphere*).

📖 Vocabulary 1

Before you read the article for the second time, have a look at some key words that are in the text. Your teacher will give you a blank strip of paper and also one of the words from the following list. Look it up in an English dictionary and copy the explanation onto the strip of paper. Don't forget to look up the form of the word (i.e. noun, adjective, verb or adverb). Then put your definition up on the wall. Look at the other definitions done by other students and match them to the correct words in your book.

1 supposedly (adverb)
2 to record information (verb)
3 the lack of (phrase)
4 a sphere (noun)
5 the equator (noun)
6 hereditary (adjective)
7 a hemisphere (noun)
8 a base (noun)
9 salinity (noun)
10 a retreat (noun)

Reading: activity 2

You have decided to give a talk to other students in your class about some of the extreme places in the world. You need to make notes in order to prepare for your talk. Read the text again and make your notes under each of these headings.

Facts about Mount Chimborazo
-
-

Problems of living on the most isolated group of islands
-
-

Facts about the Dead Sea itself
-
-

Study tip:
Vocabulary sets

When you are learning new vocabulary, it is a good idea to learn words that are related to the same idea/topic and make groups of words (sets).

For example, the words that are connected with 'temperature' could be *hot, boiling, cold, freezing, mild,* etc. This will help with your fluency when you want to write or speak about a particular topic.

Key term: spidergram

A spidergram is one of the ways you can record your vocabulary. Put the topic in the middle of the page and then write examples of related vocabulary around it.

It is called a spidergram because it looks like the body of a spider with legs around it.

Key term: cue cards

These are cards which are often used in presentations or speeches. They are used to remind you of what you want to say. They normally contain key words or topics in the correct order you want to mention them.

❝ Vocabulary 2

Vocabulary sets and related phrases

First look at the Study tip about vocabulary sets. Then work in five groups. Each group looks at one place from the reading text (e.g. the hottest place). Copy the spidergram and complete your section by adding related words that you find in the text. Then listen to the other groups and complete the other parts of the spidergram.

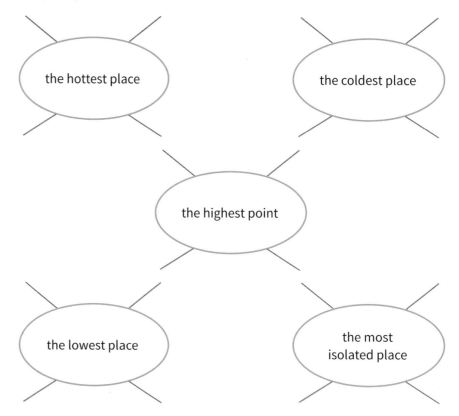

Project

Extreme places

You are going to research more about an extreme place in the world or in your country. Choose one superlative (e.g. the most populated or the wettest place). When you are researching this place, focus on these four points:

- Introduction: name and location
- Details: facts and figures
- How it compares to other places
- Any other interesting/unusual information.

Give a short presentation to the class. Remember it is always more interesting if you include some pictures in your presentation. Prepare cue cards that include such things as the main points you want to cover or some facts and figures that are difficult to remember. Try not to read your notes word for word – use your own words to present your information. Invite the other students to ask you questions at the end of your presentation.

Below is some useful vocabulary you may need in your presentation. Look at the text in the Reading section to see how to use it.

Useful vocabulary

- … which covers an area of …
- … ever recorded on the surface of the Earth
- … Not many people know that …
- … on the border of …
- … is famous for its …
- … is known as one of the … + superlative adjective (*highest, largest, tallest,* etc.)

Imagine you have been contacted by a group of young university students who want to visit the extreme place you talked about in your presentation. Write an email to them giving them some advice. In your email mention the following information:

- How to travel there
- What time of year they should go
- What clothes/equipment to take
- Interesting things to see/do there.

Language focus

Comparatives and superlatives

Analysis

Look at these phrases from the reading text and underline all the adjectives. Are these adjectives in the superlative or comparative form?

1 The highest mountain above the centre of the Earth

2 The most isolated inhabited island group

3 The lowest recorded temperature

4 The hottest temperature ever recorded on the surface of the Earth

Now look at these sentences and do the same as in the previous section. Are these adjectives in the **superlative** or **comparative** form?

5 Canada is much bigger than Switzerland.

6 The weather in the summertime is normally a bit better than in the springtime.

7 The architecture in Dubai is much more modern than in Paris.

8 People in the countryside are said to be a bit friendlier than in the city.

Work in pairs and look at the following rules about the comparative and superlative forms. Then look at the previous eight phrases and sentences to help you decide which rule is correct. Delete the wrong rule as appropriate. For each rule find an example from the eight phrases and sentences.

A Comparative forms use: *'-er' AND more … / the '-est' and the most …*

B Superlative forms use: *'-er' AND more … / the '-est' and the most …*

C One-syllable adjectives use: *'-er' AND the '-est' / more … AND the most …*

D Two-syllable adjectives that end in a consonant + *-y* use: *'-ier' AND the '-iest' / more … AND the most …*

33

E Other adjectives with two or more syllables use:
'-er' AND the '-est' / more … AND the most …

F Irregular adjectives use: *'-er' AND the '-est' / more … AND the most … / different forms from regular adjectives.*

G The definite article 'the' is used with: *the comparative form / the superlative form.*

H The preposition 'than' is used with: *the comparative form / the superlative form.*

I When we want to describe a small difference between two things, we use:
a bit / much.

J When we want to describe a big difference between two things, we use:
a bit / much.

Look at these irregular adjectives. What are the comparative and superlative forms? Use a dictionary to check your answers.

- good
- bad
- far

Practice

Exercise 1
Complete the gaps with the correct adjective form.

1 The …………………….. (wet) season of the year has just arrived.

2 I had such a good time on Saturday. Thank you for the trip. It was one of the …………………. (good) presents I've ever received.

3 I live much ………………. (far) from the station than you think. You'd better take a taxi.

4 Today it's supposed to be …………………….. (sunny) than yesterday. Let's hope the forecast is right.

5 This course is a bit ………………………………….. (difficult) than we thought, but it's good for us anyway.

6 The …………………….. (easy) part of the test was the speaking. I think I'll pass.

7 The …………………….…(beautiful) city I've ever visited was Paris. I'd love to go back there next year.

8 The …………………….. (bad) day of my life was when I overslept and missed the beginning of my science test.

Exercise 2
Look at the sentences below. They all contain a spelling or grammatical mistake. Can you spot the mistakes and correct them?

1 My sister is much beter at singing than I am.

2 People say that studying is easyer than it used to be.

3 Computers have made life more comfortabler, but also much complicated than it was a few decades ago. (2 mistakes)

4 His marks are getting worst, but he doesn't seem to worry about that at all.

5 Switzerland is one most beautiful countries I've ever visited.

6 It's becoming so much hoter then it was when I was very little. (2 mistakes)

Exercise 3

Look at the following pictures and information and discuss the differences with your partner. Make as many sentences as you can. Use both the comparative and superlative forms and *much / a bit* where possible.

A

B

Mt. Kilimanjaro – 5895 m   Mt. Blanc – 4807 m (the Alps)   K2 – 8611 m (the Himalayas)

C

The Yellow River (Huang He) – 5464 km (China)   The Danube – 2850 km (Europe)   The Ganges – 2510 km (India)

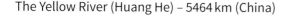

Activate your English

Work in small groups. Look at the nouns and adjectives in the tables. Compare the nouns in each section using the adjectives given in both forms: comparative and superlative.

For example: *Grammar is the most important thing about learning English. Writing is a bit easier than pronunciation.*

Discuss your opinions in your groups. For example, you may say, 'I see what you mean, but in my view pronunciation is definitely more important than grammar'.

Learning English:	important	difficult	easy	enjoyable
grammar				
pronunciation				
writing				

Food:	tasty	healthy	fattening	popular
pizza				
cheese				
broccoli				

Jobs:	stressful	hard	well-paid	rewarding
a doctor				
a teacher				
a police officer				

Idea adapted from: Grammar Practice Activities (CUP, 2006)

🔊 Listening

Pre-listening activity

Think of trips you have made and different holidays you have had.

- Where did you go?
- What did you do there?
- What sort of experience was it? Was it exciting? Was it disappointing?

Now talk to your partner about your experience.

Listening: activity 1

Listen to six speakers in track 6. What experience is each speaker describing?

See Transcript 5 at the back of the book.

Listening: activity 2

Now listen to the six speakers again. How did each person feel about the experience? Match the following statements to the correct speaker. There's one extra statement that you don't need. Before you listen, make sure you understand the words in the statements.

Speaker 1:	**A** I felt isolated.
Speaker 2:	**B** I was unprepared.
Speaker 3:	**C** I felt nervous.
Speaker 4:	**D** I want to do it again.
Speaker 5:	**E** I felt disappointed.
Speaker 6:	**F** I want to move there.
	G I felt inspired.

❝ Vocabulary 3

These are some of the words from the recording. Can you match each one to its correct definition?

a hunter *(n.)*   extinction *(n.)*   boost *(v.)*   circulation *(n.)*

immune system *(n.)*   polluted *(adj.)*   marine *(adj.)*

A It's when something stops existing. For example, when animals of the same species all die and there are no more of them.

B When something goes round.

C It's when something, such as water or air, becomes dirty. For example, when factories make the air dirty.

D It's a person who chases animals and then kills them.

E It's used when you talk about something that is connected with the sea. For example, when you talk about animals that live in the sea.

F It's the protection your body has against illnesses.

G To improve.

● Speaking

Look at some of these feelings from Listening activity 2.

A I felt isolated.

B I was unprepared.

C I felt nervous.

D I felt disappointed.

E I felt inspired.

Use the topics A–E to talk about your own experiences. First, spend a few minutes thinking about what you want to say. Think about:

- where you were
- what you were doing there
- what happened to make you feel that way
- how you feel about it now.

Now work in pairs and talk to each other about your experiences. Try to develop the conversation by asking each other extra questions about what has been said.

The phrases below will help you in your conversation.

1   When I was little I …

2   I've always wanted to …

3   I've always been fascinated by …

4   It wasn't until … (e.g. last year) that I managed to …

5   In my life I've … (e.g. done, played, read) a lot of …

6   You might think I'm crazy, but I …

7   What I never realised was that/how …

8   I've read a lot about …

 Writing

Writing: activity 1

Work in pairs and look at the following question. Can you underline the words that are important? What do you need to include in your answer? Think about how you would organise your answer, what information you could include and in what order.

In class you have been discussing the question:

How important is it for young people to travel and to get new experiences?

You feel strongly about the issue and have decided to write an article for the local magazine.

Here are some comments from other students on the topic.

I think the Internet has all the answers I need. I don't need to spend money on travelling.

I don't think that travel books, or TV programmes, can give you the same experience as when you travel to a place and experience everything with your own eyes.

Everyone should travel to different places. It is exciting and it teaches you to be independent.

The more experiences you get, the richer your life will be. You will get a lot of new ideas for your own life.

Write an article of between 100 and 150 words giving your views about this topic.

The comments above may give you some ideas, and you should also try to use any ideas of your own.

Writing: activity 2

Read the sample answer below. What are the student's views? Do you agree with these ideas? Why? Why not?

How important is it for young people to travel and to get new experiences?

When you are growing up, you hear a lot of people give you advice about what you should or should not do. Recently, I have heard that young people should travel and, of course, it came from an adult. However, how do young people feel about this suggestion? In this day and age, when the Internet is widely available and all the information you need about other countries can be found at your fingertips, is travelling something that young people should still do?

First of all, I feel that young people do need to travel. It is not only the travel itself; it is also the experience we can get out of it. I really believe it teaches you to be independent, responsible for your own actions and more organised, unless your parents always tag along and do everything for you.

Secondly, I am a big fan of the Internet. I do not think I could live without it for one single day. Also, the speed with which you can get information is breathtaking. I really cannot understand how my parents could live without it for so long. Nevertheless, getting information from the Internet and experiencing it yourself are two completely different things. For example, you read about a country experiencing a shortage of water due to a dry season. Then you visit this place. Which experience is going to stay with you longer?

Additionally, there is immense pressure on young people to decide what career path they want to take. How are you supposed to know at the age of 15 or 16? However, if you have visited a place and you felt very strongly about what you saw or learnt, this experience might help you in deciding what you want to do later in life.

Overall, I strongly believe that young people should definitely travel and experience things first-hand. If we rely on the Internet too much, the real danger is that we might start to believe that the virtual reality is our life.

Writing: activity 3

Read the sample answer again and answer the following questions.

1   Is the article formal, informal, or neutral? Why? Who is going to read this article?

2   How many paragraphs are there?

3   What do you include in the first paragraph?

4   How do you keep the readers interested?

5   What do you include in the middle paragraphs?

6 What do you include in the last paragraph?

7 How does each paragraph start?

8 Look at the following linkers and say when we use them: *first of all*, *secondly*, *additionally*, *overall*.

9 Can you find other linkers? When do we use those?

10 Can you find some phrases that mean 'in my opinion'?

🔊 Vocabulary 4

Can you find words/phrases in the sample answer that mean the same as these?

1 when you stop being a child and become an adult (phrasal verb)

2 not a long time ago (adverb)

3 anyone can get it (phrase)

4 very near and very convenient (phrase)

5 to come with you, but it's not always welcomed (phrasal verb)

6 to like very much (phrase)

7 amazing (adjective)

8 very big, extreme (adjective)

Writing: activity 4

You are going to write an article about the same issues. First, think about the organisation of your article. What ideas do you want to include and in what order? Work in pairs and discuss this. Then write your article.

Writing: activity 5

Now read your partner's article. What ideas did they include? Do you agree or disagree with them?

Read the article again and check that your partner has included the following:

* at least three paragraphs
* a rhetorical question
* their own opinion
* linkers to start paragraphs
* linkers to join sentences
* an example to support their opinion.

Is there anything they need to work on a bit more?

What about their grammar, vocabulary, spelling and punctuation? Did you notice any mistakes?

Summary

Can you remember …

- in what country the coldest inhabited place on Earth is?
- **three** interesting facts about the Dead Sea?
- which word or phrase is the odd one out: *a peak, a mount, below sea level, altitude*? Why?
- what these four words mean: *a sphere, the equator, a hemisphere, salinity*?
- what the comparative and superlative forms are for these adjectives: *good, heavy, difficult, far*?
- what the mistake is in the following sentence? 'My bag is much more new than yours.'
- how to use comparative adjectives correctly? Can you write **three** sentences comparing yourself and your friend? Use 'a bit' and 'much' in your sentences.
- who/what inspired one of the speakers in the listening section?
- the **two** adjectives, from the listening vocabulary section, that are used when a) air or water becomes dirty, and b) talking about things connected with the sea?
- **two** linkers that mean 'and' and **two** linkers that mean 'but'?
- **one** phrase that means 'I think'?
- how to list ideas for and against? Describe **two** advantages and **two** disadvantages of travelling on your own. Use the correct linkers to introduce your ideas.
- how to keep readers interested when writing an article?

Progress check

Go back to the Objectives at the beginning of this chapter and assess your progress. Use the symbols below to show how confident you feel about your learning progress.

I am very good at this.	✓ ✓
I am OK, but I need a bit more practice.	✓
I can't do this yet and I need to look at this section again.	✗

Chapter 4:
The life of an astronaut

Objectives

In this chapter, you will learn and practise:

- reading skills – answering questions about being an astronaut
- speaking skills – discussing the topic of space and being an astronaut
- listening skills – completing sentences about becoming an astronaut
- reading and writing skills – reading a short text about becoming an astronaut and filling in a form.

You will also learn and practise the following language skills:

- compound nouns
- prefixes
- modal verbs and other phrases of obligation
- the use of capital letters and punctuation marks.

You will 'Activate your English' by:

- discussing a wide range of topics using precise vocabulary
- discussing the requirements for different jobs.

Chapter 4: **The life of an astronaut**

📖 Reading

Pre-reading activity

Have you ever thought what it would be like to be an astronaut in space? What would daily life be like?

Work in small groups and discuss the following everyday routines. What are these routines like for an astronaut in space on board a space shuttle? What difficulties do you think astronauts face?

Discuss the following:

- sleeping
- brushing teeth
- eating
- exercising.

Reading: activity 1

Read the text and find the answers to the questions in the pre-reading activity. In pairs, compare the information with your original ideas. What do you find strange or surprising?

Living in space

A typical day for an astronaut in space is a very busy one. On top of astronauts' working hours spent on duties like routine maintenance of equipment or doing scientific experiments, a lot of the time is dedicated to their personal daily routine. Everyday tasks that might seem simple on Earth have to be approached quite differently in space.

Sleeping

The International Space Station orbits the Earth, which means that astronauts on board experience 15 sunrises in a day. Of course, it is impossible for them to follow this cycle, as humans are used to a 24-hour day, so all astronauts' schedules are fixed to follow the 24-hour cycle. Eight hours are allocated for sleeping, but most astronauts will only sleep for six because of their long working day. Astronauts can choose where they want to sleep, but the key to getting a good night's rest is to strap their body to their bed, so that they don't float around while sleeping. Astronauts sleep in sleeping bags which are tethered to the walls. There are a few brave individuals who go to sleep while floating free, but they are very likely to be woken by bumping into something. Another thing that is very different from Earth is the constant noise made by all the machines on board and the light. That is why some of the crew prefer to use earplugs and eye masks to help them sleep. For the astronauts, the day on board the International Space Station begins at 6 o'clock GMT*.

Daily hygiene

Zero gravity makes daily hygiene quite a challenge. There are no showers or taps on board. Instead astronauts Iclean their faces and hands with wet towels and waterless shampoo is used to wash their hair. The advantage of waterless shampoo is that it doesn't produce any foam, so there is no need for rinsing. After astronauts have brushed their teeth, they swallow the toothpaste and the water they use for rinsing. When astronauts shave using electric shavers, they do this next to a fan which sucks in all the hairs.

Eating

Space food has improved quite a lot since the first space missions. In the early 1960s, space food was stored in aluminium tubes in small bite-sized pieces. It was done this way so that the food containers wouldn't weigh too much or be too large to store. The range of space food for astronauts to choose from expanded in the 1970s. Nowadays, plastic containers are used to store food and astronauts have a choice of around 150 different kinds of food. Many ready-made meals are dehydrated meaning water has to be added to them before the food can be consumed. Astronauts can then heat up their meals in ovens, just like we do on Earth. No extra care needs to be taken when eating fruits and vegetables, but liquid foods, like soups, need to be eaten carefully. Therefore, astronauts use straws to sip the food from packets. Bread may also cause problems because any loose crumbs floating around in zero gravity can cause damage to equipment, or they can be breathed in by astronauts. For this reason, astronauts eat specially prepared tortillas which don't make so many crumbs. Another interesting fact is that astronauts who stay in zero gravity for a long time, tend to complain that a lot of food starts to taste bland as their taste buds become less sensitive. So, it is no surprise that spicy food proves popular with many astronauts.

Exercising

Floating in zero gravity means that astronauts use their muscles less than on Earth, so the muscles weaken. Complete weightlessness also affects astronauts' bone density (how strong their bones are). To prevent both of these problems daily exercise is very important, so the International Space Station is equipped with treadmills and special exercise bicycles without wheels. Another benefit of daily exercise is that astronauts are prepared for when they return home and experience gravity again.

*GMT is Greenwich Mean Time. The Greenwich Meridian Line in England is the place where all time zones are measured.

44

Reading: activity 2

In Chapter 2 you learnt how important it is to try and guess the meaning of words from the context. To remind yourself what to look out for when guessing the meaning of new words, read the Study tip box about guessing vocabulary by looking at the context in the Vocabulary section of Chapter 2.

Look at the words that are highlighted in blue in this text. Can you guess their meaning? Read the sentences around them and make a note of your guesses. Use easy words to explain the meaning.

Compare your ideas with a partner. Do you have similar explanations? What helped you decide?

Vocabulary 1

Exercise

Look at the following definitions of the highlighted words and match them to the correct words in the text.

A to schedule time for a particular activity (verb in the passive voice)

B to increase in number or size (verb)

C when you don't get enough water into your body (adjective)

D when something is attached to something else so that it doesn't move (verb in the passive voice)

E to wash something out, usually with water, to make it clean (verb)

F small bits of bread that fall off when you are eating, or cutting, bread (noun)

G when something moves through the air or water without falling or sinking (verb)

H when you suck in small amounts of liquid with your mouth (verb)

Reading: activity 3

Read the text again and answer the following questions.

1 What work commitments do astronauts have in space?

2 How long do astronauts tend to sleep for?

3 Why do some astronauts find it difficult to sleep in space? Give **two** details.

4 Why is waterless shampoo used in space?

5 What types of food could cause problems when eaten on board a spacecraft? Give **two** examples.

6 Why do some astronauts like to eat spicy food?

7 Why is it important for astronauts to exercise in space? Give **two** details.

Did you know?

- 547 people had gone into space by the year 2014.
- Astronauts can become up to 5 cm taller when they have been in space for at least a month.
- As it doesn't rain or get windy in space, an astronaut's footprint can stay on the Moon for at least 1 million years.

Speaking

Discuss the following points in small groups.

- What do you find fascinating about the daily routine of an astronaut? Why?
- What would you find difficult if you were an astronaut in space? Is there anything from Earth that you would miss if you were in space?
- What hobbies would you not be able to do in space?
- Would you ever consider becoming an astronaut? Why? Why not?

Project

Imagine you are going into space for a long time. You are allowed to take five personal items. What would you take with you and why? First, think very carefully about your selection. Then, discuss your choices in small groups.

Imagine that you have been asked to carry out a survey to find out what young people of the 21st century think are the ten most important and useful things in our lives. Interview students from other classes and make notes of the most common answers. Discuss your findings in small groups and make your final top ten selection. Then tell the other groups/students in your class. Don't forget to give reasons why these things were chosen.

Have a class discussion about '**What your generation will be remembered for**'. Consider future inventions and discoveries in different areas of life.

- Based on the information from your survey, write a report about what things young people can't live without in everyday life. At the end of your report, say whether you think these things are essential for life, or if young people have become too dependent on these.

Key term: compound nouns

In English we can make new nouns by putting two words together. For example, when you put **foot** and **ball** together, you get **football**. These are called compound nouns.

Sometimes these words are written as one word, sometimes they need a hyphen, and sometimes they are written as two words. For example, *toothpaste, a passer-by, a bus stop*.

If you are not sure how to write a compound noun, check in an English dictionary.

Vocabulary 2

Compound nouns

Exercise 1

There are a number of **compound nouns** in the reading text. Scan the text and find examples of compound nouns that are written as one word and two words.

Exercise 2

Work with a partner and look at the following words. Join the correct halves together to make a new compound noun. Now listen to track 7 and check your answers. Only two compound nouns are written as two words. Which ones are they?

Can you think of other compound nouns starting with these words? Check your answers in the dictionary.

1	white	shuttle
2	wheel	line
3	drinking	shine
4	rain	board (2x)
5	space	book
6	face	ball
7	basket	water
8	bank	scraper
9	chop	sticks
10	dead	fall
11	gold	chair
12	key	fish
13	pick	pocket
14	sky	note
15	sun	

See Transcript 6 at the back of the book.

Exercise 3 – pronunciation
Listen to the compound nouns from Exercise 2 again and repeat them. Can you mark the **syllable stress**? Where is the syllable stress in compound nouns?

Activate your English
Complete the gaps with words from Exercise 2 and then discuss the answers in small groups.

1 Does a …………………….. make a good pet? What pets do you have? Is it important for a child to have a pet? Why? Why not?

2 Do you think tablets, like iPads, without …………………………. are popular? What is your prediction for the future of computers? In what form will they exist?

3 Do you have a …………………………. account? What are the advantages and disadvantages of having a …………………….. account and what sort of information is it OK to share?

4 Do you think there is enough ………………………. access in public buildings in your town/city? Is it easy for …………………….. users to use the public transport? What changes would you suggest if you were the mayor in your town/city?

5 Do you think we'll still be paying with …………………………. in ten years' time? What means of payment will we have then, in your opinion?

6 Is it good to have ………………………….? Can you meet your ………………………., or are you often late with giving in your homework, assignments or project work?

Key term: syllables

When you say words in English, they are divided into syllables. For example, when you say '**pro-nun-ci-a-tion**', this word has five syllables, but only one is stressed.

Knowing which syllable in the word is stressed helps you with pronunciation.

Key term: syllable stress

In English one syllable in a word is always stressed. That means that this syllable is said more strongly. This stress can sometimes move to a different syllable.

For example, in '**re**-cord' the first syllable is stressed when it's a noun, but when it's a verb the second syllable is stressed: 're-**cord**'.

Study tip: Syllable stress and new words

When you are learning new words, mark the stress of these words. It is important to use the correct pronunciation of new words right from the beginning.

You can look up the stress in an English dictionary. Online dictionaries have recorded pronunciation.

The pronunciation in dictionaries is shown between two forward slashes, like this: /prəˌnʌnsiˈeɪʃn/. The main stress is often marked as a small line similar to an apostrophe('). The stressed syllable is the one that comes after this small line. In the word 'pronunciation' the fourth syllable is the one you stress most when speaking.

Key term: prefixes

Prefixes are the part of a word that is sometimes added at the beginning. Prefixes are often added to adjectives and verbs, but some nouns can have prefixes too.

Some prefixes make the word negative. For example, *kind* and **un***kind*.

Other prefixes add a new meaning to the original word. For example, *national* and **multi***national*. 'Multi' here means 'more than one'.

Key term: hyphen

A hyphen is a short line that connects two words together. Compound adjectives are commonly joined by a hyphen. For example, *hard-working*.

---

7   What advice would you give to tourists not to be a victim of …………………………? Are you always careful with your things when travelling? What precautions do you take?

8   Everyone has the right to have access to …………………………………. . Do you think that sometimes people waste a lot of …………………………? Can you think of some examples?

9   Can you think of any well-known …………………………? Do you have any in your country? Do you think …………………….. are the answer to the lack of housing in some countries? Would you like to live in one? Why? Why not?

10 How do you see the future of learning? Do you think we'll still have …………………………. to write on in the classroom in future? Do you think all learning will be interactive and students will study from home? What would the advantages and disadvantages of interactive learning online be? Would you personally enjoy it?

📖 Vocabulary 3

Prefixes

Exercise 1
Read the information about **prefixes** in the Key term box. There are four words with prefixes in the reading text. Can you find them? Which word has a prefix that makes the word negative? Which words have a prefix that adds a new meaning? What is the meaning of these prefixes?

In this chapter you are going to learn about prefixes that add a new meaning to the original word.

Exercise 2
Your teacher will dictate a few more words. Work in three groups and focus on one prefix. Listen to your teacher and write down the dictated words that can be used with your prefix.

bi	pre	de

Exercise 3
Look at these six columns. The words in each column need the same prefix. Can you identify the prefix? Which of these prefixes usually need a **hyphen**?

A	B	C	D	E	F
war	confident	paid	paid	violent	war
graduate	service	eat	developed	resident	social
script	portrait	complicated	value	smoking	clockwise
production	discipline	sleep	cooked	judgemental	perspirant

Exercise 4 – meaning
Look at all the prefixes from Exercises 2 and 3 and match them to their correct meaning:

1 too much

2 not enough

3 it only involves you, not other people

4 after something happens

5 before something happens

6 two

7 to remove

8 against

9 absent from something

Exercise 5 – pronunciation
Listen to the words with prefixes in track 8 (recording 1). Where is the stress? Do we ever stress prefixes? Can you write them in the correct column?

Now listen to the answers in track 8 (recording 2). Were you correct? Listen again and copy the pronunciation. Pay attention to the syllable stress.

○ ○ ⬤	○ ⬤ ○	○ ⬤ ○ ○	○ ○ ⬤ ○

See Transcript 7 at the back of the book.

Activate your English
Rewrite the following questions using one of the words from Exercises 2 and 3. Then answer these questions in pairs.

1 Do you think it's important to speak two languages these days? Why? Why not?

2 What do you know about the issue of forests being cut down in order to use the land in other ways? Can you think of examples of how this affects the area and the living things there?

3 How popular is ready-made supermarket food in your country? How healthy do you think it is?

4 In what jobs are people not paid enough or paid too much? Can you give some examples and explain why you think that?

5 Are there problems with people behaving in an unfriendly way (e.g. playing loud music on the bus, graffiti, etc.) in public places in your country? How do you think these people should be punished?

6 Do you agree with the idea that all public places should be smoke-free? What benefits does it bring?

7   In your opinion, do astronauts need a lot of personal discipline? Why?

8   Have you ever slept too long and been late for something? When?
    What happened next?

🔊 Listening

Pre-listening activity
Work in small groups. Discuss whether you have heard of any famous astronauts. What facts do you know about these astronauts?

Listening: activity 1
Listen in track 9 to the first part of a talk on the radio given by an astronaut called Tim. Listen for his personal details. Don't write anything down. How many details can you remember?

Listening: activity 2
Read the profile of an astronaut and try to predict the type of answer you will need.

Listen to the whole programme and complete the profile. Write one or two words only in each gap. You will hear the talk twice.

Profile of an astronaut

Personal details

Tim Mason
a He comes from ....
b He first worked as a ....

Facts about the Space Center

c Johnson Space Center* was founded in ....
d A total of .... astronauts trained at the Space Center were from outside America.

Training

e The .... was the main difficulty for Tim.
f Taking the swimming test without .... meant he had to repeat it.
g Tim was most pleased with how .... his mentor was.
h Tim has chosen to be a .... when his training has finished.

*US spelling.

Speaking

Discuss the following questions in small groups.

- What do you think you would find difficult about the astronaut training?
- What would you enjoy?
- What type of person makes a good astronaut?

See Transcript 8 at the back of the book.

Language focus

Modal verbs and other phrases of obligation

Analysis

Read about **modal verbs of obligation** in the Key term box. Then look at Transcript 8. The modal verbs and phrases have been highlighted for you.

Key term: modal verbs of obligation

Modal verbs have a lot of different meanings.

Modal verbs of obligation, or lack of obligation, are used to talk about rules. This means how necessary, or not, it is for you to do something.

Modal verbs are, for example, **can**, **should**, **must**, **have to**.

Put the modal verbs in Transcript 8 into the following four categories:

A   It is necessary for you to do something

B   It is a good idea for you to do something

C   You are allowed to do something

D   It is important that you don't do something.

Look at the phrases and modal verbs in the transcript again and how they are used in sentences. Decide which ones need to be followed by the bare infinitive, without 'to' (i.e. *do*), and which ones need the infinitive form, with 'to' (i.e. *to do*). List them under the following two headings.

- **Modal verbs and phrases without 'to'**
- **Modal verbs and phrases with 'to'**

Look at the following groups of sentences and decide if they mean the same. Then answer the questions about their meaning.

1   You <u>can</u> be 5 minutes late. You <u>can't</u> be late. You <u>mustn't</u> be late.

In which sentence(s) are you allowed to be late?

2   You <u>must</u> do your homework before I get back. As a student you <u>have to</u> do your homework.

In which sentence(s) is it necessary for you to do your homework?

3   You <u>can't</u> touch any of the exhibits. You <u>mustn't</u> touch any of the exhibits.

In which sentence(s) are you not allowed to touch the exhibits?

4   In our school you <u>have to</u> wear a uniform at school; you get into trouble if you don't. In some countries you <u>don't have to</u> wear a uniform at school.

In which sentence is it necessary to wear a uniform?

In which sentence is it not necessary to wear a uniform?

5   You <u>should</u> see the doctor; you don't look too well. You <u>must</u> see the doctor; this could be something more serious.

In which sentence is the obligation stronger?

Practice

Exercise 1
Work in pairs and fill in the gaps with the most suitable modal verb or phrase. Sometimes more than one answer is possible.

1   Astronauts .... complete three stages of special training.

2   Trained astronauts .... choose what assignment they want to work on.

3   Students .... be on time for their lessons.

4   When you go and see a movie, you .... talk on the phone during the movie.

5   You .... eat or drink during your lessons.

6   You .... get up early on your day off.

7 You .... take an exam at the end of your studies.

8 You .... use your mobile phone in class.

9 Passengers .... show their passports and tickets before boarding the plane.

10 You don't look well. You .... see the school nurse.

Exercise 2

Work in pairs and write down ten sentences about your school rules. These rules could be about, for example, uniforms, mobile phones, lateness, exam preparation, etc.

In your rules you can include what is **necessary** to do and what is **not allowed**.

Then compare your lists and say why you selected these ten rules. How important are these rules in your opinion?

For homework, choose a public place (e.g. a cinema, a hospital, a library, etc.) and write down ten rules for this place. In your next lesson, read out the rules to the class without saying what place it is. Your classmates will have to guess what place you chose to write about.

Activate your English

Work in small groups. Look at the selection of different jobs below. Discuss what obligation, or lack of obligation, each job involves and explain why. For example, an astronaut has to be physically strong because the training is very tough.

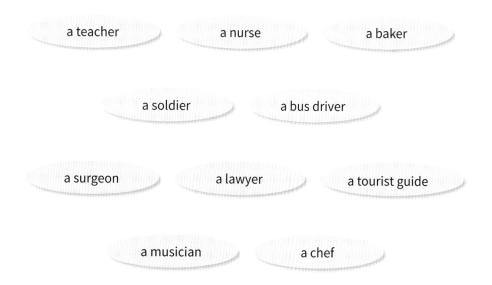

a teacher   a nurse   a baker

a soldier   a bus driver

a surgeon   a lawyer   a tourist guide

a musician   a chef

Reading and ✍ writing

Reading: activity 1

You are going to read a text about Alessio. His dream is to become an astronaut. Read the first two paragraphs quickly and find as many personal details about Alessio as you can. Then work with a partner and write down these details.

Alessio's full name is Alessio Francesco Grossi. His family came to America from Italy many years ago and settled down in Chicago, in the state of Illinois. They used to live at 73 Morgan Street, but moved just before Alessio was born and now they all live together at 4 Ashland Avenue. Alessio was born in the United States 19 years ago on 17th September 1996. His younger sister was born in the same month, but three years later in 1999.

This year Alessio is busy preparing for his final exams at his local college. He has chosen Science, English and Maths for his finals. Apart from English he can also speak Italian and would like to learn Spanish. After his holiday in Italy next year, he intends to study Computer Science and Chemistry at the University of Chicago. His dream is to train at the Johnson Space Center and to become an astronaut. That is why he wants to apply for a place on a programme for young hopefuls, which provides some basic training and preparation for young people like Alessio.

Alessio is quite a private person, so he doesn't like it when people keep calling. He is much happier if people email him rather than call him on his cell phone. That is why he keeps his email address quite simple so that everyone can remember it. It is alessio1@hotmail.com. His cell phone number is 078 602 9937. Alessio takes his dream very seriously. If he manages to complete this programme, it will teach him very useful skills and give him a lot of self-discipline that will help him in all sorts of jobs. It will also look good on his curriculum vitae. He's very hard on himself. He goes to the gym three times a week and goes running in the park twice a week. On top of that, he goes swimming every Saturday. He is very fit and his Physical Education teacher thinks Alessio is the best student he has ever had, with an excellent fitness level. Alessio thinks that if you have the chance to go on this programme, six months are just not enough. That is why he would like to attend for one year.

Study tip:
Filling in a form
Read the form very carefully. Make sure that you answer in the way the form asks you to do. Watch out for words such as 'circle', 'underline', 'tick' and 'delete'. It is also important that you use capital letters correctly.

When you are looking for information in the text, underline the answers so that you can find them again later.

Make sure that you complete the form in the first person (i.e. *I*, *my*, etc.).

Reading: activity 2
Look at the following words on the left that are often found on forms. Can you match them to their examples on the right?

1 delete	A 15 ⟨188⟩ 21
2 tick	B I would like to attend a ~~part-time~~/full-time course
3 underline	C blue and green
4 circle	D September March <u>June</u>
5 give details	E Yes ☐ ✓ No ☐
6 use capital letters	F MARIA CALERRI

Reading: activity 3
You are going to complete a form based on the information about Alessio. Look at the form to see what information is required. Then read the text very carefully and underline the information. Imagine you are Alessio and fill in the form with the correct information.

Training programme for young astronauts

Section A

Full name: _____

Gender (please delete): male/female

Address: _____

_____

_____

Date of birth: _____

Mobile/Cell phone number: _____

Email address: _____

Preferred method of contact (please tick):

Phone ☐   Email ☐   By post ☐

Section B

Languages spoken: _____

How would you describe your level of fitness (please circle):

poor   average   good   excellent

Preferred length of course (please delete):

six months/one year

Section C

In the space below, write <u>one</u> sentence giving your reason for choosing this programme, and <u>one</u> sentence giving details of how this programme would help you in your future studies/career.

_____

_____

_____

_____

_____

_____

Writing: activity 1

Look at the following categories of words. Circle the ones that need a capital letter.

days	first names	months	school subjects
common nouns	surnames		parts of the day
names of cities	shops	pronouns	street names
countries	nationality	languages	

Writing: activity 2

Read the Key term box about **punctuation**. With a partner, look at some examples of punctuation and what we call it in English. Can you match the names and the punctuation?

A	a capital letter	.
B	an exclamation mark	,
C	a full stop	H
D	an apostrophe	?
E	a question mark	!
F	a comma	It's

Writing: activity 3

Look at the following sentences. What punctuation marks can you find? When do we usually need to use them?

1 What's your name?

2 I've never eaten seafood, lamb or avocado.

3 Peter! Wait!

4 If you don't study hard, you'll fail your exam.

5 This is Katie's coat. She must have forgotten it.

Writing: activity 4

With a partner, find the mistakes in punctuation in the following sentences and correct them.

1 Ive told you many times. (1 mistake)

2 Can i ask you what time it is. (2 mistakes)

3 If i were you I wouldn't do it (3 mistakes)

4 She want's to be an astronaut. (1 mistake)

5 I want to go to tokyo New york and paris. (4 mistakes)

Writing: activity 5

In the form-filling exercise, you have to write two sentences at the end of the form. Look at the following question.

Write one sentence about why you want to study English in Oxford and one sentence about your previous experience of studying English.

The following answers are not correct. Work with your partner and say what types of mistakes the student made. In each answer there are two types of mistakes. Then rewrite the sentences so that they are all correct.

1   I like Oxford. I study english in china for two years.

2   I heard that Oxford is a beautifull city and there are very good langage schools. My brother studyed there last year and really enjoyed himself. I've ben studying Englih for four years now and want to continu my studys in the UK to improve my pronunciation. I find pronunciation really dificult and need a lot of practice.

3   Marta want's to study in Oxford because, her sister live's there and she want's to be near her She studied English at primary school a long time ago, but only for three years

4   because my friend was there and liked it very much. i've been studying english by myself on the Internet and by watching american films.

Writing: activity 6

Answer the following three questions. Remember what you have learnt in this section and write your answers very carefully. Then check your answers with your partner.

1   Write one sentence giving details of the course you want to study, and one sentence saying why you chose it.

2   Write one sentence giving details of a part-time job you want to do, and one sentence explaining your reasons.

3   Write one sentence explaining the main reason why you want to study in Australia, and one sentence saying how you found out about our college.

Summary

Can you remember …

- how astronauts sleep?
- which verb is connected with movement: *to expand, to float, to sip*?
- which word(s) are connected with water: *crumbs, dehydrated, to rinse, to sip*?
- what a compound noun is?
- how to make a compound noun with 'rain', 'gold' and 'bank'?
- **four** prefixes, what they mean and give an example with a word for each of them?
- where the syllable stress is in: *oversleep, postgraduate* and *self-discipline*?
- **three** words that need a hyphen?

- where the Johnson Space Center is?
- **two** things astronauts have to do during their training?
- **three** words/phrases that mean the same as 'must'?
- how to talk about rules? Make **three** sentences about rules in your school.
- the difference in meaning between 'You mustn't come on Friday' and 'You don't have to come on Friday'?
- in what 'person' you should fill in a form?
- when we use capital letters in English? Give **five** examples.
- what each of these is called?   **?   ,   '   !   .**
- how to use the punctuation marks from the previous question? Can you use the marks in sentences?

Progress check

Go back to the Objectives at the beginning of this chapter and assess your progress. Use the symbols below to show how confident you feel about your learning progress.

I am very good at this.   ✓ ✓

I am OK, but I need a bit more practice.   ✓

I can't do this yet and I need to look at this section again.   ✗

Chapter 5:
Social media

Objectives

In this chapter, you will learn and practise:

- reading skills – taking notes about the advantages and disadvantages of social networking sites
- speaking skills – discussing the issue of social networking sites
- listening skills – multiple-choice exercise about the impact of social networking sites
- writing skills – writing a summary about the advantages and disadvantages of social networking sites; writing an article expressing disadvantages.

You will also learn and practise the following language skills:

- sequencing linking words
- words and phrases connected with computers and social networking sites
- first conditional and other future clauses.

You will 'Activate your English' by:

- discussing future intentions
- developing and maintaining a dialogue.

Chapter 5: Social media

📖 Reading and ✏️ Writing

Pre-reading activity

In this chapter we are going to talk about social media, especially social networking. Discuss in groups whether you use social networking sites. Think about the advantages and disadvantages of using these sites. Choose one member of your group to write down the ideas you think of during your discussion.

Compare your ideas with the other groups.

Reading: activity 1

Work in two groups. One group reads Article A which looks at the advantages of social networking and the other group reads Article B which looks at the disadvantages. Read the text and underline the positive and negative points that are mentioned.

When you have finished reading, compare the information with your partner. Then tell somebody from the other group what you found out about your topic.

ARTICLE A

The advantages of social networking

The main reason why most people sign up to social networking sites is to stay in touch with other people. These sites also help people to <u>find their childhood friends</u> that they have lost touch with. <u>Renewing these long-lost friendships</u> is just a click away. It is very exciting to be able to <u>catch up with friends</u> and <u>keep up with their news on an almost daily basis</u> thanks to frequent updates.

Keeping up-to-date, however, doesn't have to be restricted to friends and acquaintances. What many people tend to forget is that they can also use networking sites for professional reasons. It is actually a great way of finding out about upcoming job opportunities. Friends might know about job vacancies that may not be advertised elsewhere or they can even recommend their friends for certain jobs. Even people already employed can promote their business online. This is particularly important for artists, actors and musicians who can create pages devoted to their band or theatre company, and inform fans about their gigs or latest exhibitions. In addition, the sites can be used to allow the public to give instant feedback on the artists' work and to interact with their favourite artist.

Another great plus of social networking sites is how easy it is to organise an event with your friends. Thanks to different settings people can organise their friends by different criteria. These criteria could be how close friends they are, common interests and hobbies or where they live. This means if a certain event takes place, for example, an open-air concert or a football match, all they have to do is invite the right group of friends to attend. Some networking sites offer a range of quizzes and games, so friends living on opposite sides of the globe can invite each other to participate and compete in a variety of games without leaving their homes.

ARTICLE B

The disadvantages of social networking

Sadly, social networking is not always good for us. One of the biggest drawbacks is how much easier it has become for your personal details to be accessed online. The dilemma people are faced with is how much to share. On the one hand, if people don't share information, their potential friends won't be able to find them. On the other hand, if people share too much, they risk that this information will be found by dishonest people and used to their own advantage. They can then target people with endless junk mail or hijack their email accounts. In the worst cases, this can even result in attempts to access people's bank accounts or to steal their identity.

Another big online threat is people known as 'scammers'. They operate on social networking sites and trick the users into downloading malware, which is harmful software. People may download it and be totally unaware of what it really is. For example, someone could receive a link to a video clip which looks absolutely genuine. The trick is, however, that if people want to watch the clip, they are asked to install a program, which is, in fact, a virus. After the computer has been infected with the virus, the scammers access the person's friend list and try to send the malware to their friends too.

After joining a social networking site, it can become overwhelming, as well as addictive for people. All of a sudden, the friend list can grow from just a few to hundreds, in some cases even thousands. This means a lot of constant updates. Unless people customise their settings, they will be bombarded with numerous feeds, links and posts and these will make it very difficult to find specific information about friends they are really close to. The number of constant updates also means that people find it very tempting to keep checking, just in case there is something they need to know. This will only distract them from whatever they are doing.

All in all, we can say that the advantages of having a social networking account outweigh the disadvantages. However, it goes without saying that the key to online safety is to be sensible and cautious when deciding what information and how much to share online.

🔊 Vocabulary 1

Look at the following words and phrases that appear in the texts. Scan your text and circle the words. Can you guess the meaning from the text? What do you think the words mean? Then check in an English dictionary. Explain the meanings to a partner.

Article A	Article B
• to catch up with friends (phrasal verb)	• a dilemma (noun)
• to keep up with the news (phrasal verb)	• to be faced with something (phrase)
• to find out (phrasal verb)	• to use something to your own advantage (phrase)
• upcoming job opportunities (adjective)	• genuine (adjective)
• to be devoted to something (phrase)	• overwhelming (adjective)
• instant feedback (adjective)	• tempting (adjective)

Key term: topic sentences

A topic sentence is a sentence in a paragraph that introduces the topic of that paragraph. This sentence will tell you what topic is discussed and it is often near the beginning of the paragraph. Everything that is written after the topic sentence supports the topic, usually by giving examples or explanations.

Reading: activity 2

You are going to make notes for a presentation about the advantages of social networking. First look at the Key term and Study tip boxes about **topic sentences** and note-taking. Then look at Article A about the advantages of social networking. The topic sentences have been highlighted for you. Can you find examples of

Study tip:
Reading and note-taking
When you are asked to read a text to identify an idea, it is a good idea to look for a topic sentence in each paragraph. This helps you when you need to locate particular information. You should look for topic sentences to know if the paragraph contains the information you need in order to answer the question. Make sure you write brief answers under the correct heading.

the supporting ideas for each topic sentence? Read the text and underline this information. The first paragraph has been done for you as an example.

When you have finished, check in pairs to see if you have the same information.

Reading: activity 3

Prepare a presentation about the advantages of using social networking. Copy the notepad below and complete the notes with the information you have found. Make your notes under each heading.

Do this activity in pairs and then compare with the rest of the class.

The most common reasons given for joining social networking sites.

- ....
- ....
- ....

How social networking sites can help people to look for work.

- ....
- ....

What types of outdoor social activities can be arranged online.

- ....
- ....

Reading: activity 4

Now you are going to do the same as in activity 3, but this time look at the disadvantages of using social networking sites. Before you start, remember the steps you took to find the information for Article A. Now work on your own and complete the notes for Article B about the disadvantages.

The dangers of revealing too much personal information online.

- ....
- ....
- ....

What damage scammers can do.

- ....
- ....

Consequences of constant updates.

- ....
- ....

Key term: summary

A summary is a piece of writing that reduces a long text to a much shorter one. In the summary, the writer selects the most important information from the original text and rewrites it.

**Study tip:
Writing a summary
(core level)**

After doing a note-taking type exercise, you write a summary. This summary is based on the text you read for your note-taking. You can use your notes, but you can also use other ideas from the text. However, you must make sure that you write about things related to the question.

It is very important that you:

- use correct grammar
- express the ideas from the text in your own words
- use linking words to join the ideas together
- write concisely and keep to the word limit.

Writing: activity 1

You are going to write a **summary** about social networking based on your notes. First read the Key term and Study tip boxes about how to write a summary.

Look at the question:

> Imagine that you have given a successful presentation to your classmates. Your teacher wants you to write a summary for students who couldn't attend the talk.
>
> Look at your notes in Reading: activity 3. Using the ideas in your notes, write a summary about **the advantages of social networking**.
>
> Your summary should be about 70 words long (and no more than 80 words long). You should use your own words as far as possible.

Look at the summary below written by a student and answer the following questions.

1 How does the student introduce the topic?

2 Is the introduction too long? Why? Why not?

3 What ideas does the student include?

4 Can you find examples of the words/phrases that the student used to paraphrase ideas from the original text?

5 How could the summary be improved?

> Social networking sites have many advantages. These sites give us the opportunity to rediscover friends we thought we had lost. We can follow what our existing friends do every day. People can look for a job on these sites. Our friends might know what jobs are going to become available. They can suggest us for jobs to other people. If you want to go out with your friends, it is easier to invite them.   (74 words)

Writing: activity 2

The words below are missing from the summary. Look at the three examples of sequencing linkers and insert them into the summary in activity 1.

First of all,

Moreover,

Finally,

Writing: activity 3

Work with a partner and look at some more examples of linkers below. Can you match them to their synonyms in activity 2?

furthermore / last, but not least / to begin with / what is more / also / firstly

Writing and Speaking: activity 4

Work in groups of three. You are going to give a short talk on one of the following topics.

Topics:

> The advantages of learning English

> The disadvantages of being famous

> The advantages of shopping online

Think of four points to include in your talk and prepare some written notes to help you.

Now give a short talk to your group. Try to include four ideas and use four sequencing linkers from activities 2 and 3 to connect the ideas.

Writing: activity 5

Write a summary about the disadvantages of social networking.
Look at the question:

> Imagine that you have given a successful presentation to your classmates. Your teacher wants you to write a summary for students who couldn't attend the talk.
>
> Look at your notes in Reading: activity 4. Using the ideas in your notes, write a summary about **the disadvantages of social networking**.
>
> Your summary should be about 70 words long (and no more than 80 words long). You should use your own words as far as possible.

Writing: activity 6

Exchange summaries with your partner and check what ideas they included. Now look at the checklist below. Read your partner's summary again and check it against the points on the summary checklist.

Summary checklist

- There is an introduction to the topic.
- Examples of the drawbacks of social networking are included.
- The summary is about 70 words long.
- The summary includes sequencing linkers.
- The summary includes some paraphrasing.
- The correct grammar is used, so that the text is easy to read.
- The correct spelling and punctuation are used.

63

🔊 Vocabulary 2

In Article B, 'The disadvantages of social networking', there are words connected with computers and social networking. First look back at the Study tip box about vocabulary sets in Vocabulary 2 in Chapter 3.

In a group, scan the text and try to find as many words connected with the topic as possible. One example for each vocabulary set has already been added for you.

junk mail — 'computer words' with negative meaning

download — words connected with activities you can do on the computer

friend list — words connected with social networking sites

💬 Speaking 1

Discuss the following points in small groups. Try to use some of the words/phrases from Vocabulary 2.

- Do you have an account on a social networking site?
- How long have you had it?
- What made you open this account?
- What are the benefits of being on a social networking site?
- Have you ever noticed any drawbacks?
- Do you think there should be an age restriction for joining these kinds of sites? Why? Why not?
- What information do you share on your site? Do you think you shouldn't share this type of information?
- What else do you use the site for?
- Do you think you spend too much time on social networking sites? Give examples.

Project

You are going to research how much time young people in your school spend on the computer and what they mainly use it for. You are also going to compare two different age groups.

In groups, prepare a questionnaire. Also, decide what age groups you want to interview.

When you have finished your survey, prepare a chart with your findings. On your chart, compare the two age groups. Then report back to the class. Have a discussion about your findings.

- Were your findings surprising? Why? Why not?
- Do you think people at your school spend too much time on the computer?
- What do people use the computer for most of the time?
- Do people use the computer to do their homework?
- Do people use a lot of different social networking sites?

Using the information from your survey and your chart, write a report to highlight the differences in the uses of computers by the two age groups. At the end of your report, suggest improvements or recommend changes to the way these two groups use computers.

✚ Language focus

The first conditional and other future clauses

Analysis

Look at the examples of the first conditional below. Study these examples and then answer the questions.

- If you join every social network and add hundreds of people as friends, you'll receive updates constantly.
- If you share too much, you may discover that someone else is pretending to be you.
- If the social network is popular, you may be able to track down old friends and acquaintances and renew long-forgotten friendships.

1   Do we use the first conditional to talk about the future or the present?

2   Is there a **real** possibility that something will happen?

3   How many clauses does a first conditional sentence have?

4   What tense do we use in the 'if clause'?

5   What tense, or type of verbs, do we use in the 'main clause'? (The main clause is the part without 'if'.)

6   Which clause do we use to make a question: the 'if clause' or the 'main clause'?

7   Does a conditional sentence always have to start with the 'if clause'?

8   Do we need to separate the clauses by a comma?

Other linkers: Look at some more time linkers that follow the same rules as 'If sentences'.

as soon as   **when**   **until**   **unless**   **before**

Look at the following sentences using these linkers and underline the verbs in both clauses. What are the tenses / verb forms used?

1   As soon as I get there, I'll phone you.

2   When he finishes his homework, he's going out with his friends.

3   Until you tell me the truth, I can't help you.

4   Unless it's very cold, we're going for a walk near the lake tomorrow.

5   I'll come to say goodbye before I go home.

Meaning:
Study the following pairs of sentences. Is there a difference in meaning between the two linkers? Can you explain the difference?

A   <u>When</u> I get there, I'll phone you. / <u>As soon as</u> I get there, I'll phone you.

B   <u>Unless</u> it's very cold, we're going for a walk near the lake tomorrow. / <u>If</u> it's <u>not</u> too cold, we're going for a walk near the lake tomorrow.

C   <u>Until</u> you tell me the truth, I <u>can't</u> help you. / <u>When</u> you tell me the truth, I <u>can</u> help you.

D   <u>If</u> you want, I can lend you my dictionary for the day. / <u>When</u> you want, I can lend you my dictionary for the day.

Practice

Exercise 1
Can you put the verbs in the brackets in the correct form?

1   If it .... (not rain) on Friday, I .... (go) for a walk.

2   Unless he .... (decide) not to go, we .... (meet) outside school at two.

3   Until we .... (have) more information, we .... (can't/finish) this project.

4   What .... you .... (do) if he .... (not come)?

5   Before you .... (open) a Facebook account, you .... (should/talk) to your friends about their experiences.

6   When you .... (hear) from your sister, ... you .... (can/tell) her that I need to speak to her?

7   She .... (be) very disappointed if you .... (not come) to the party.

8   He .... (might/leave) his job unless he .... (get) a pay rise.

Exercise 2

Complete the sentences with your own ideas.

1   I'll phone you as soon as …

2   If I see you tomorrow, I …

3   You can go out after you …

4   Before you leave the classroom, … you …?

5   When this school year finishes, I …

6   If I pass the exam, I …

7   Will you let me know as soon as you …?

8   He might become ill if he …

9   She'll visit us before she …

10   They'll go to the cinema after they …

Activate your English

In small groups, look at the incomplete sentences below. Try to complete the sentences with your own ideas and tell each other about your future plans. Develop your answers into a dialogue with your partner.

Before I leave the house tomorrow, …

After I leave this school, …

As soon as the lesson is finished, …

When I'm in my twenties, …

If I get good marks in my IGCSEs, …

If I get rich one day, …

 Listening

Pre-listening activity

You are going to listen to a radio programme about research into social networking sites and the use of the Internet. One of the points discussed is the impact of using the Internet on the relationship between young people and their grandparents.

Before you listen, look at the three pictures. In small groups, discuss what you imagine the findings might be. In what way do you think the relationship between young people and their grandparents may have changed? What do you know about the generation gap?

Listening: activity 1

Listen to the first part of the programme in track 10 and compare your ideas with the ideas mentioned in the radio programme.

🎧 Vocabulary 3

Before you listen for a second time, look at these words from the listening text. What do they mean? In pairs, look up one of the words or phrases in an English dictionary. Then explain the meaning to the class.

1 pastime (noun)

2 to have an <u>impact</u> on something/somebody (noun)

3 upbringing

4 computer <u>savvy</u> (adjective)

5 grown-ups (noun from a phrasal verb 'to grow up')

6 to play an invaluable role in something (phrase)

7 to broaden somebody's horizons (phrase)

8 empathy (noun)

9 a <u>reliable</u> source (adjective)

10 to run out of time (phrasal verb)

Listening: activity 2

Look at these multiple-choice questions and find the key words. Listen to the whole programme and choose the best answer, A, B or C.

1 **What are the experts concerned about?**

   A   The number of teenagers using social networking sites.

   B   The problems that long-term use of social networking may bring in the future.

   C   The dangers connected with the Internet.

2 **In the past, grandparents**

   A   didn't have any access to the Internet

   B   brought up their grandchildren instead of the parents

   C   used to teach their grandchildren a lot of useful skills.

3 **These days teenagers**

   A   use the Internet to find answers

   B   buy a lot of smartphones and tablets

   C   think that their grandparents can't answer their questions.

4 **What do the majority of grandparents think?**

   A   Their grandchildren like them less.

   B   Their grandchildren don't visit them any more.

   C   Their grandchildren don't ask them about the past.

5 **How can the generation gap be improved?**

    A   Grandparents should own the latest devices.

    B   Grandparents should improve their knowledge of technology.

    C   Grandparents should use a computer more for the latest entertainment.

6 **Who is much busier these days?**

    A   parents and teenagers

    B   only the teenagers

    C   only the parents

7 **According to research, most parents believe that**

    A   they should choose their child's passwords

    B   they should control everything their child does online

    C   they can best decide when their child joins social networking sites.

8 **A recent study has shown that children want**

    A   help with their homework

    B   help when something goes wrong

    C   to have open discussions with their parents.

See Transcript 9 at the back of the book.

> **Study tip:**
> **Writing an article**
>
> When you are asked to write an article, you need to discuss a certain topic providing supporting ideas.
>
> You can provide supporting ideas which are both positive and negative. This type of article is called **balanced**.
>
> However, you can also choose to include only positive ideas, or only negative ideas. This type of article is called **one-sided**.

Writing

Writing: activity 1

In the Reading and Writing section in this chapter you read two articles. Look at the Study tip box about writing an article. Now look back at Article B about the disadvantages of social networking. Is this article balanced or one-sided?

Writing: activity 2

Look at the highlighted words in Article B. Why do we use them? Can you match these words to their correct language function below?

1   Introducing an idea

2   Adding more ideas

3   Expressing contrast

4   Giving an example

5   Giving two examples at the same time

6   Making a conclusion

Speaking 2

Choose one topic from the selection below. Spend a few minutes thinking about what you want to say. Then tell your partner your opinion. Try to follow the outline in Writing activity 2 and use as many linkers and phrases as you can.

The topics are:

- The drawbacks of mobile phones
- The drawbacks of using Facebook
- The drawbacks of watching too much TV
- The drawbacks of downloading music/films
- The drawbacks of online courses
- The drawbacks of living in the countryside
- The drawbacks of living in a big city

Writing: activity 3

Choose one of the topics from the previous Speaking activity and write your article for a school magazine. Your article should be 100–150 words long. When you have finished, read your answer again to make sure the spelling, punctuation and grammar are correct.

Summary

Can you remember …

- **three** advantages and **three** disadvantages of social networking sites?
- what these three words/phrases mean: *to catch up with somebody, dilemma, overwhelming*?
- what a topic sentence is and why it is important?
- **two** synonyms for 'moreover' and one synonym for 'finally'? Can you make sentences with these?
- **two** words connected with computer activities?
- what is wrong with the following sentences? 'If he go back home by bus, I join him.' / 'When I'll have my next holiday, I might go to the seaside.'

- how to complete these sentences? 'If the weather's nice tomorrow, …' ; 'As soon as I get home today, …'
- the words that mean: 'to have a good knowledge of computers'; 'to have no time left'; 'a free-time activity'?
- the difference between a balanced and a one-sided article?
- a phrase you can use for your conclusion in articles?

Progress check

Go back to the Objectives at the beginning of this chapter and assess your progress. Use the symbols below to show how confident you feel about your learning progress.

I am very good at this.	✓ ✓
I am OK, but I need a bit more practice.	✓
I can't do this yet and I need to look at this section again.	✗

Chapter 6:
Art traditions

Objectives

In this chapter, you will learn and practise:

- reading skills – answering questions about totem poles and henna; extracting information from graphs and charts
- speaking skills – discussing the topic of art
- listening skills – completing sentences about the history of face painting; listening to four short recordings and answering questions
- writing skills – writing a letter to a friend describing a photograph, including correct language and content.

You will also learn and practise the following language skills:

- phrases to give yourself time to think
- active/passive voice
- collocations and fixed expressions.

You will 'Activate your English' by:

- describing a piece of art.

📖 Reading

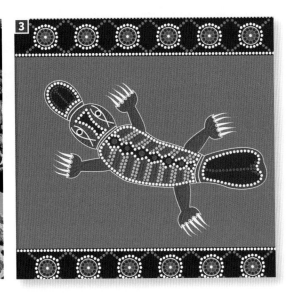

Did you know?

- The largest totem pole collection in the world is located in British Colombia in Canada.
- On average, a totem pole takes between 3 and 9 months to make.

Pre-reading activity

How much do you know about different art around the world? Look at the pictures of types of art from different parts of the world. Can you name the type of art and the country or the continent it originated in?

Discuss in groups whether you like this kind of art. Why? Why not?

Is there any art specific to your country or region?

Reading: activity 1

Scan Texts A and B opposite and find out the type of art in each text, and where it originated from. Remember that you don't need to read the whole article, and stop reading as soon as you find the answer.

SURVIVING ART TRADITIONS

Text A

Native American Indians expressed themselves through their artwork, which is carved onto totem poles. Many people believe that all Native American Indian tribes carved totem poles, but this is far from the truth. Carving totem poles was a tradition among many tribes, especially those that lived along the Pacific coast where forests grew. However, those Native American Indians who lived in the south-west and the plains, and Inuit Indians, did not have trees to carve. The height of totem poles can vary considerably. Long ago totem poles were found to stand around 12 m tall. Today, Native American Indian artists continue to carve trees, but some totem poles are short and are used in homes as decoration. Traditionally carved totem poles involve a great deal of work, craftsmanship and time to produce. As a result, an authentic pole will cost more than $1500 per metre.

The raising of a totem pole is an important celebration among the Indian tribe. A hole is dug for the pole to stand in. The pole is carried to the site in a ceremony which often hundreds of people attend. Ropes are used to raise the pole into place. Singing and dancing to drums accompanies the pole raising. Often poles are raised this way before the carving begins.

Many people believe that totem poles are religious symbols, but this idea is false. Rather than acting as religious symbols, carvings represent the tribal nation and convey the tribes' history. The story of a totem pole is frequently passed down from generation to generation. Having the story documented in this way helps keep this tradition recognised in our history.

Totem poles held messages from the people who carved them. Carvings were symbols that may tell a story about the carver, such as his position not just in his own family, but also within the tribe. Carvings such as an eagle could symbolise pride in his tribe. Often traditions and tribal life were combined in the decorations carved into the pole. These days, many

totem poles no longer exist because of decay and rot. However, there are still some tribes that continue to practise this ancient art form, and these totem poles are still being enjoyed by collectors of tribal art.

Text B

The art of henna (called 'Mehndi' in Hindi and Urdu) has been practised for over 5000 years in Pakistan, India, Africa and the Middle East. Some documentation has been found relating to this art form that it is over 9000 years old. Because henna has natural cooling properties, people of the desert have been using it for centuries to cool down their bodies. They make a paste with henna and soak their palms and the soles of their feet in it to get an air-conditioning effect. They feel its cooling sensation throughout the body for as long as the henna stain remains on their skin. Originally, it was noticed that, as the stain faded away, it left patterns on the surface of the skin which led to ideas for making decorative designs. In ancient Egypt, mummies were decorated with henna designs and it is documented that Cleopatra herself used henna as decoration. Henna was used not only by the rich, but also by the poor, who could not afford jewellery and so used henna to decorate their bodies.

Henna, scientifically named *Lawsonia Inermis*, is a shrub that grows up to 3.5 m high. It can be found in countries with a hot climate, such as Egypt, Pakistan, India, Africa, Morocco and Australia. The plant grows best in heat up to 50 °C and it contains more dye at these temperatures. It wilts in temperatures below 10 °C. It also grows better in dry soil rather than damp.

The henna plant contains lawsone, which is a reddish-orange dye that binds to the keratin (a protein) in our skin and safely stains the skin. The colour of the stain can range from pale orange to nearly black depending on the quality of the henna and how well it adapts to the texture of the skin. A good henna, fresh from hot and dry climates, will create the darkest stain. Henna also acts as a sunblock, and helps to prevent the sun's harmful rays from damaging the skin, so there is an added benefit to having henna designs in the summer.

www.indians.org/articles/totem-poles.html

http://silknstone.com/pages/About-Henna.html

Henna

	Plant	Leaves	Flowers	Seeds
Description	greyish-brown bark	almond-shaped	creamy white	brown when ripe
Use	tool handles and tent pegs	skin and hair dye	medicine, oil for perfumery	medicine, oil for perfumery

Did you know?

- Henna applied to your hands tends to fade away in one or two weeks.
- People in rural areas of North Africa use small twigs from henna shrubs as toothpicks to keep their teeth and gums healthy.

🔊 Vocabulary 1

Guessing unknown words from the context

Exercise 1

Work in two groups, A and B. Look at the words and phrases highlighted in blue. Can you guess their meaning?

To help you remember how to guess unknown words from the context, look back at the Study tip box in Chapter 2. Use a dictionary to look up any words that you are unsure of.

When you have finished, compare your ideas with other students in your group.

Then exchange information with the other group until you know the meanings of all the highlighted words.

Exercise 2

Match each word/phrase to its correct definition in the table below.

Text A	Text B
1 Groups of people with common traditions. (noun) 2 Large areas of land that are flat. (noun) 3 To give information to somebody. (verb) 4 When something gets worse naturally over time. (verb) *(two possible answers)* 5 A space in the ground. (noun) 6 The good feeling you have when you have achieved something. (noun) 7 To give knowledge of something to somebody younger. (phrasal verb) 8 To cut into a piece of wood in order to produce decorative patterns. (verb)	1 Parts of your body that touch the ground when you walk. (noun) 2 To become less visible or clear. (phrasal verb) 3 A thick bush. (noun) 4 To attach itself to something. (phrasal verb) 5 To put something into liquid and to leave it there for some time. (verb) 6 When plants become dry and bend. (verb) 7 A mark that is left, very often when you spill liquid. (noun) 8 Something that is used to change the colour of something, for example hair or fabric. (noun)

Reading: activity 2

Read the two texts carefully and answer the following questions. Don't forget to underline the answers when you find them.

A Why did south-western and Inuit Indians not carve totem poles?

B Why are authentic Indian totem poles expensive? Give **two** reasons.

C What do people do during the celebration of the totem pole raising? Give **two** details.

D What information did the carvers put onto the totem poles? Give **two** examples.

E Why did poor people start to use henna for decorative purposes?

F What are the best conditions for the henna plant to grow in? Give **two** examples.

G What is the extra advantage to using henna in the summer?

H According to the table, which parts of the plant have healing qualities?

Reading: activity 3

Look at the 'study tip' box about graphs and charts. Then look at the following graphs and charts and answer the questions.

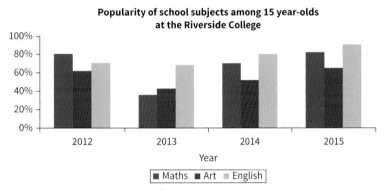

Popularity of school subjects among 15 year-olds at the Riverside College

1 In which year was English the most popular among students?

2 In which year was art the least popular subject?

3 Which subject was the most popular in 2012?

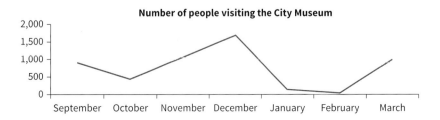

Free time activities

4 According to the pie chart, which is the most common free time activity among boys?

5 Which is the least common free time activity among girls?

6 Is reading more common among girls or boys?

Number of people visiting the City Museum

> **Study tip:**
> **Graphs and charts**
>
> In some reading exercises you will be asked to interpret or explain information taken from a diagram which could be a table, a graph or a chart. The information in these diagrams is often written as a number or a percentage.
>
> Look at the information on the graph/chart and at the same time at the *legend* (i.e. the note/explanation) which tells you what the numbers, percentages or colours mean.

7   According to the graph, when did most people visit the City Museum?

8   Which two months were least busy?

9   How many people visited the City Museum in March?

 Speaking

Speaking: activity 1

Giving yourself time to think

Sometimes when you have to discuss a topic that you are not very familiar with, you may need some time to think before you answer or make a comment. Here are some expressions to use to give you thinking time. Look at them and complete the missing words.

1   I haven't really ……………….. about that.

2   Let me ……………….. .

3   Oh, that's a …………………. question.

4   How can I ………………. this?

Listen to the expressions in track 11 and check your answers (Transcript 10).

Listen again and mark the stressed word. Try to explain why these words are more important than the others.

Then practise saying the expressions.

Speaking: activity 2

In small groups discuss the following questions. If you need a few seconds to think, use one of the phrases from activity 1.

- Do you like art? Why? Why not?
- What sort of art do you like?
- Do you think graffiti is art or an act of vandalism?
- Is art important in everyday life? Give examples.
- Should art be taught at school? Why? Why not?
- Do you think it is easy to be an artist these days? Give reasons.
- Do you ever go to galleries or museums to see art? When did you last go? Did you enjoy it?
- What are the art traditions in the region where you come from?
- Do you feel it is important to preserve art and art traditions? Why? Why not?
- How can art make our lives richer?

Project

In this chapter we are talking about visual art. Think about a painting or a photo that you know and like very much, or that is very special to you.

If you can, bring a copy of it to school and tell your classmates about it.

- Describe what is happening in that picture/photo.
- If it is a painting, say where/when it was painted and who painted it.

Study tip:
Pronunciation – sentence stress

In spoken English we tend to stress some words in a sentence more than others. We do that to show the listener which words are important.

For example, '*I would **never** do that.*' We stress 'never' because we focus on emphasising the negative 'not at all'. But if we say '*I would never do that*', we mean: I wouldn't do that, but another person might.

- If it is a photo, say where/when it was taken and who took it.
- Explain why you chose it.
- Describe how it makes you feel.

 # Language focus

Active or passive?

Analysis

In Chapter 2 you learnt about the passive voice and how and why we use it in English.

1 Can you give an example of the passive voice?

2 Look at the two sentences below taken from Text A and underline the verb forms. How are they different?

3 Which sentence uses the passive voice and which one is in the active voice?

4 In which sentence is the subject active? (The subject of the sentence is the person who did the activity.)

5 In which sentence is the subject passive? (Another person did the activity.)

Many Native American Indians expressed themselves with their artwork …

Ropes are used to raise the pole into place.

Scan read Text A and look for more examples of the passive and active voice. When you find them, underline them.

Then look at your examples with a partner and answer the following questions.

1 In which examples (passive or active voice) are we more interested in what happens?

2 In which examples are we more interested in the person who did something?

3 Which voice, active or passive, is slightly more formal and impersonal?

4 In which writing genres do we often use passives?

5 Which voice, active or passive, is more suitable for situations when you talk or write to a friend about what you did?

Practice

Exercise 1

Look at the following sentences. Are the verb forms in the passive voice or the active voice? In some sentences there is more than one verb form.

1 He's gone home.

2 This picture was painted a long time ago.

3 I painted my room light green.

4 It'll be done as soon as we can.

5 She was running down the street when she saw him.

6 I want to be corrected every time I make a mistake.

7 I corrected all the mistakes in my homework.

8 I haven't done the washing up yet.

9 It's done very quickly.

10 She's done something silly again.

Exercise 2
Do you need the active or the passive voice? Complete the gaps with the correct verb form.

1 As she .... (look) at the photo, she .... (remember) that it .... (take) by her father.

2 The gallery .... (build) in the 1990s and the work .... (fund) by the local council.

3 The last exhibition .... (put) together by our students who .... (work) very hard on it to make sure it was ready for the big opening.

4 The living room .... (paint) white because we .... (think) that this colour would make the living room look bigger.

5 Every day hundreds of students .... (come) to our museum to see the latest exhibition of North American totem poles.

6 Our exhibition .... (see) by hundreds of people every week.

7 The film .... (show) three times a day at the cinema.

8 We .... (try) to encourage more young people to take up art as a subject in schools.

9 Students should .... (encourage) to express their ideas in a creative way.

10 The plane .... (take off) any minute now.

11 The house .... (damage) quite badly during the last earthquake.

Exercise 3
Look at the first paragraph in Text B. It tells us about how people used henna in the past and the uses for henna nowadays. Is this paragraph mostly written in the passive or the active voice? Why?

With a partner, rewrite this paragraph using passives where possible. When you have finished, swap your answers with another pair and check their answers. Are they grammatically correct? Who managed to use more passive verb forms?

Activate your English
For homework research some traditional art. This could be decorative (e.g. jewellery, masks or pictures) or everyday art (e.g. pottery, carpets or traditional costumes). Write a short paragraph to include the following information.

- Where and when it started.
- How it is made.
- What people used it for in the past.
- If it is still used and what for.
- If it has any special meaning.

- If it is used during any special celebration/event.
- What happens during this celebration.

Read your paragraph to the class without saying what type of art you are describing. Instead of saying the name, use the pronoun 'it' or 'they'. Other students have to guess what your paragraph is about.

🔊 Listening 1

Pre-listening activity

You are going to listen to a radio talk about face painting and how it has been used throughout history. With a partner, try to think of as many examples of face painting as you can. Think of different occasions or reasons why people paint their faces. Write your ideas down.

Listening: activity 1

Listen to the talk (track 12). How many uses, does the radio programme mention? What are they? Did you have the same examples? Did you have examples that are not mentioned?

💬 Vocabulary 2

Here are some words from the listening. Do you know what they mean? Check the meaning of these words in an English dictionary.

- to camouflage yourself (verb)
- hunting (noun)
- to blend in (phrasal verb)
- to sneak up on (phrasal verb)
- to enable somebody to do something (verb)
- to enhance something (verb)
- wrestling (noun)
- to participate in (verb)

Listening: activity 2

Listen again to the programme and fill in the sentences below with the missing details. Before you listen, look at the notes and try to predict the type of detail missing from each gap. Then listen and complete the gaps. Use one or two words in each gap.

A brief history of face painting

Face painting has a very long history.

a Face painting is not only a .... activity for children. It is used more widely.

b To avoid being seen in the ...., people would paint their faces when hunting.

c Some tribal warriors added .... on their faces because they wanted to scare their enemy.

Ceremonies

d People thought they would have .... if they painted their faces a certain colour.

Entertainment

e Opera performers used face painting to improve their ....

Sport

f .... uses face painting to give the participants the right image.

g Nowadays, the .... also paint their faces in some sports.

Growing popularity

h After .... face painting became popular with children.

See Transcript 11 at the back of the book.

🔊 Vocabulary 3

Exercise 1

Transcript 11 includes a number of collocations and fixed expressions. To help you remember what a collocation or a fixed phrase is, look back at Chapter 2.

Can you find the missing word to complete the collocations/fixed phrases below? Read the transcript and try to find these as quickly as possible.

1   to think ....

2   to date ....

3   a .... variety of

4   to be aware ....

5   good ....

6   would be .... likely to do something

7   in the .... environment

8   to .... common

9   to be associated .... something

10 to participate ....

11 it wasn't .... about the 1980s

12 as a .... for somebody to enjoy themselves

Exercise 2

Look at the expressions in Exercise 1 and try to identify the words used in each phrase. For example, verb plus preposition.

Exercise 3

In pairs, rewrite the following questions with the most suitable phrase from Exercise 1. Then choose three questions to ask other students.

A   What will you probably not do this weekend?

B   What started happening in your life after you joined this school?

C   What are your views on modern art?

D   What do you need to be careful about when living in a big city?

E   What is art useful for?

F   Do you take part in creative projects? Give examples.

Writing

Pre-writing activity

You are going to write about your favourite photograph. Look at the four photos above chosen by other students.

- Why do you think they chose them?
- Why do you think they are special to them?
- Try to guess when and where they may have been taken.
- What is happening in each one?

Writing: activity 1

Read the task and the sample answer written by a student called Arturo. Did he choose one of the four photos above or a different photo?

When you read his answer, underline the information which corresponds to the three bullet points. Arturo made some mistakes. Don't worry about those at this point.

> You have recently taken up photography as your hobby. You entered a competition at school and one of your photographs won the first prize. You want to write to your friend about the photograph.
>
> **In your letter you should:**
>
> - say where and when it was taken
> - describe the photograph
> - say why you chose it for the competition.
>
> You may use one of the photos above, or you may write about a photo of your own.
>
> Your letter should be between 100 and 150 words long.

Hi Simon,

Hope everything is good your end. Sorry I'm not in touch for so long, but I was really busy with my photography obsesion and with the school photography competition.

You'll never believe this, but I was winning the competition. One of my photos won the first prize. I was really thriled because I don't expect that at all, to tell you the truth.

Anyway, let me tell you about the photo. I took it last month when I have visited my friend Takeshi. I'm sure I told you about him. We studied English together in Malta and then stayed in touch. He invited me to stay with him and his grandmother. She's in the picture, actually. I took it one afternoon outside their house. The grandmother had this crazy cat which kept jumping on people's sholders. Plus, each of the cat's eyes had a diferent colour. I never see anything like it. They made a funny pear. The grandma looks happy in this photo and the cat looks really grumpy. I thouht the photo showed the mood of the two quite well and that's why I felt it would stand out in the competition. What do you rekon?

Apart from that, nothing much had happened. What about you? Any news?

Take care and drop me a line when you can.

Arturo

Key term: content

When we talk about content, we mean the information and ideas that you write about in your answer. This does not include the grammar or the vocabulary.

Writing: activity 2

When your writing is marked in exams, it is assessed for **content** and language. With a partner, look at the areas of assessment below and discuss whether they relate to content or language.

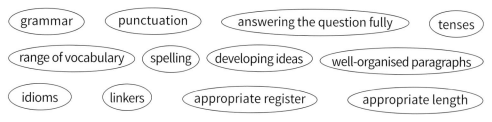

grammar punctuation answering the question fully tenses

range of vocabulary spelling developing ideas well-organised paragraphs

idioms linkers appropriate register appropriate length

Writing: activity 3

Look at Arturo's letter again. His English is good, but there some areas he needs to improve. Which ones are they?

Underline the mistakes and correct them.

🔊 Vocabulary 4

In your writing, try to include a wide range of interesting and appropriate vocabulary. Arturo is good at this and uses a variety of different words and phrases. Read the letter again and find the words that have the same meaning as the following words/phrases and definitions. Compare your ideas with a partner.

1 a strong interest in something (noun)

2 This may surprise you, but … (phrase)

3 very excited (adjective)

4   to be honest (phrase)

5   a linker used when you want to change the topic in your letter (adverb)

6   to continue to write to somebody even though you don't see them (phrase)

7   also (conjunction)

8   This is the first time I've seen something like this. (phrase)

9   in a bad mood (adjective)

10   What is your opinion? (phrase)

11   write to me (phrase)

Writing: activity 4

Now you are ready to write your letter. Write an answer to the same task as in activity 1. Either choose one of the four photos in activity 1 or write about another one that you have taken.

Try to include some of the new vocabulary in your letter.

When you have finished, read your letter again to check that you have answered all the points. Also, proofread your work and try to correct any language mistakes.

Writing: activity 5

Swap your letter with a partner. Read your partner's letter and discuss together which areas from activity 2 are strong points and which areas, in your opinion, could be improved.

🔊 Listening 2

Listening: activity 1

You are going to listen to four recordings in track 13 and answer two questions for each recording. Look at the questions first and highlight key words.

Then listen and write down the correct answers. Write no more than three words for each answer.

You will hear each recording twice.

Questions:

1   **a**   When does the east wing reopen?

    ....

    b   On which day is the gallery closed to the public?

    ....

2   **a**   Who told the man about the café?

    ....

    b   What will the woman have in the café?

    ....

3   **a**   Which photography exhibition does the man want to see?

    ....

    b   How much will the man have to pay for the ticket?

    ....

4 a What time will the girls have to leave the museum tomorrow?

....

b Which exhibition will they be able to see?

....

See Transcript 12 at the back of the book.

Listening: activity 2

In listening exercises there is often distracting information to test your listening for detail. For example, when you are asked 'what time' there might be two different times given, but only one will be correct for that question.

Here are the distractors from Listening activity 1. Why are they not the correct answers? Listen again and explain why. Compare your answers with a partner.

- Question 1(a) – two weeks, June
- Question 1(b) – every Thursday
- Question 2(a) – my girlfriend
- Question 2(b) – banana cake, sandwiches
- Question 3(a) – modern photography
- Question 3(b) – $7.60
- Question 4(a) – 2.30, 8 p.m.
- Question 4(b) – famous Hollywood dresses

Summary

Can you remember …

- **three** types of traditional art from around the world?
- which words, from the following selection, go with 'totem poles' and which ones with 'henna'? The words are: 'a hole', 'soles', 'shrub', 'plains', 'decay', 'to wilt' and 'to fade away'.
- **two** phrases you can use to give yourself more time to think when you are discussing something?
- why we use the passive voice in some situations rather than the active voice? Give **two** reasons.
- how to change sentences in the active voice into the passive voice? Can you rewrite the following sentences in the passive voice? 'I'm going to clean my room tomorrow.' 'I took this photo last month.'

- **three** examples of situations when people paint, or painted, their faces?
- what prepositions you need in the following collocations: 'to think…….'; to date………..'; 'to be aware …….. something'?
- what you are assessed on in the written exercises in the exam? What are the two categories?
- at least one example for each category in the previous question?
- what you should do when you have finished your writing?
- the words that mean: 'in a bad mood'; 'a strong interest in something'?

Progress check

Go back to the Objectives at the beginning of this chapter and assess your progress. Use the symbols below to show how confident you feel about your learning progress.

I am very good at this.	✓✓
I am OK, but I need a bit more practice.	✓
I can't do this yet and I need to look at this section again.	✗

Chapter 7:
Sports and games

Objectives

In this chapter, you will learn and practise:

- reading skills – answering questions about sports
- speaking skills – discussing the topic of sports and games and keeping fit
- listening skills – multiple choice about the history of the Paralympics
- reading and writing skills – reading a short text about keeping fit and filling in an application form for a gym.

You will also learn and practise the following language skills:

- vocabulary sets – types of sport and related vocabulary
- verb forms.

You will 'Activate your English' by:

- participating in a questionnaire
- presenting and comparing results.

Chapter 7: Sports and games

📖 Reading

Pre-reading activity
Look at the pictures above.

- Do you know the sports?
- Which one looks the most exciting? Why?
- Which one looks the most dangerous? Why?
- Which one looks the most difficult? Why?
- Have you ever tried any of them yourself?
- Which one would you like to try yourself?
- Are these sports played in your country?

Reading: activity 1
What do you think the sports in the pictures have in common? Look at the title and read the introductory paragraph in the text to find out. What do you think 'bidding for a place' in the title means? Check your ideas in pairs, then with the class.

THE SEVEN SPORTS BIDDING FOR A PLACE IN THE SUMMER 2020 OLYMPICS

Each Olympic Games we see some sport disciplines being dropped, or reinstated, and some completely new ones being introduced. In February 2013 the International Olympic Committee met at its headquarters in Lausanne, Switzerland, to decide which of the seven sports initially applying to take part in the 2020 Tokyo Summer Olympics should be included. Let's take a look at these sports, which are hoping to join the other Olympic disciplines.

Inline speed skating

Inline skating evolved from roller skating. This sport is believed to have its roots in Northern Europe where, during warm months, frustrated ice-skaters missed skating on ice. Inline skating has recently become extremely popular in urban areas thanks to its health benefits. With inline skating, you can burn as many calories as with running, but this sport is much gentler on your joints.

Inline skaters race either on roads, or on track circuits, and the races are very similar to cycling. The Annual World Championships include races that range from 200 m to a marathon. If the Olympic bid is successful the races would range from 300 m to 15 km, but would exclude the marathon.

Karate

Japan has given us this very popular type of martial art. The competition consists of two participants trying to score points using a range of techniques, such as kicks, sweeps and punches. The two competitors fight on a special mat called a tatami and they try to target the opponent. The part of the body they can strike is anywhere above the belt except the throat. The judges then award points based on, for example, the correct distance between the two competitors, their sporting attitude, timing, the application of techniques, etc.

Despite its popularity worldwide, karate has not been an Olympic discipline in the past and has been rejected three times before.

Softball and baseball

Historically, softball was based on baseball, so naturally there are some similarities to this sport, for example they both use a bat and a ball. Despite the name softball, the ball is quite hard and it is also bigger than the one used in baseball. The bat used in softball is shorter and the game is played on a pitch that is smaller than a baseball pitch.

The Olympic bid is a joint one for both sports. However, this wouldn't be the first appearance of these sports at the Olympics. Women's softball was part of the Games between 1996 and 2008, but was dropped from the 2012 Games together with men's baseball. Men's baseball has a longer Olympic history, with its first entry in 1904. Since then it has appeared at the Games several times. To become reinstated, men's baseball has to tackle one obstacle—the absence of professional players. This factor is vital to its success in the Olympic bid.

Sport climbing

Sport climbing is a type of rock climbing, but the difference is that permanently fixed anchors are used so that climbers don't have to worry about fixing these to the wall while climbing. For this reason, the risk of falling is greatly reduced and the climbers can focus on the performance side of the climb and try to get as high as possible.

This is a relatively new sport and enthusiasts are hoping it will be an Olympic discipline in the near future.

Squash

Squash has a long history. It is thought to have existed in various forms for about 140 years. The game can be played by two or four players who have to take it in turns to hit a small, hollow rubber ball with a racket. The aim is for the ball to hit the front wall below a marked line. If a player misses the ball, the opponent scores a point.

The World Squash Federation has been trying to make squash an Olympic discipline since 1992. The sport failed to gain inclusion in the 2012 London Olympics. History repeated itself when it lost its bid to rugby and golf for the 2016 Olympics in Rio.

Wakeboarding

Wakeboarding developed from water skiing in Australia in the 1980s. The participant uses a board, called a wake, which is often towed by a boat, but can also be pulled by a cable system or trucks. The participant slides across water while performing a series of acrobatic moves like jumps and flips.

The Olympic bid is for cable wakeboarding and, as the name suggests, cables attached to machines are used to pull a maximum of nine riders. Each of these riders then has to perform a variety of tricks without falling.

Wakeboarding enthusiasts claim that they have been trying to get this exciting sport included in the Olympics for the past 40 years.

Wushu

Wushu is a type of martial art that comes from China and, at one point, kung fu and wushu were considered the same sport. However, wushu has developed into a combination of performance and martial arts. In wushu the emphasis is on speed, power and natural movement. Wushu competitions are held in two main categories; the moves, called 'taolu', and the full contact fighting, called 'sanda'. Only the former is proposed for the 2020 Olympic bid. It is also the category in which participants are allowed to used spears and swords. Participants perform their routine and are awarded points, but these are deducted for any mistakes that appear during the performance.

One of the most famous wushu practitioners is Jet Li, who went on to become a film star. Amongst his most successful films are *Romeo Must Die* and *The Expendables*.

Did you know?

The youngest female Olympic gold medallist was 13-year-old Marjorie Gestring from the USA. She won her gold medal for the 3 m Springboard Diving event in Berlin in 1936.

🔊 Vocabulary 1

Look at the highlighted words. Before you look them up in an English dictionary, try to guess the meanings from the context. The questions below should help you to guess.

Introductory paragraph

- reinstated – What does the prefix 're-' mean?

Inline speed skating

- have its roots in – What follows this phrase? Is it a person, a time or a place? Do you know what the word 'root' means?
- exclude – Read the second paragraph. Is there a word that means the opposite to 'exclude'? Does 'exclude' have a positive or negative meaning?

Softball and baseball

- joint – Look at the whole sentence. How many sports are we talking about?
- tackle one obstacle – Read the whole sentence. What is the obstacle? Are we talking about something positive or negative? Read the last sentence in this paragraph. Do we want to keep the situation the way it is, or change it?

Sport climbing

- anchors – What are they attached to? What are they used for?

Squash

- inclusion – This is a noun. Can you think of the verb? Read the whole sentence. What were they trying to achieve?

Wakeboarding

- is often towed by – Read the whole sentence. What/who is towed? What is used to tow? There is also a synonym in the second half of the sentence. Which word is it?

Wushu

- the former – Read the previous sentence. How many categories are mentioned? Which category does 'the former' refer to?
- are deducted – Do you get more points or do you lose points? How do you know?

Reading: activity 2

Read the article again and answer the following questions. Before you start reading, look at the questions and circle the key words. Do you need to read everything in order to answer the questions?

1 Why is inline skating a good way of keeping fit?

2 Which part of the body is not allowed to be hit during a karate competition?

3 How does softball differ from baseball? Give **two** details.

4 What might prevent baseball from appearing at the Olympic Games?

5 What minimises the chances of a possible accident while sport climbing?

6 What will be used to tow the wake at the Olympics?

7 Which type of wushu uses weapons?

Q Speaking

Speaking: activity 1

Imagine you have been asked to choose three sports from Reading activity 1 that should be included in the 2020 Olympic Games. Work in small groups and discuss which three sports you would like to include and why. For example, how interesting the sport is for people to watch or what you can learn from the sport, etc. When you have chosen your sports, compare your three choices with the other sports.

Speaking: activity 2

In small groups, discuss the questions below.

- What is your favourite / least favourite sport? Why?
- Do you think it is a very dangerous sport? Explain your opinion.
- Do you know if it is one of the Olympic sports?
- Is your country good at this sport?
- What sport is the most popular in your country?
- Can you think of any sports that are unusual in your country? Why are they unusual?
- Do you like team sports? Why? Why not?
- Do you take part in a sport yourself? Which one? How often?
- Do you think that young people should do more sport? Why?
- What can young people learn from participating in sport? Give examples.
- What sports are practised at your school?
- Do you think that enough time is spent on physical education at school? Why? Why not?

🔊 Vocabulary 2

Can you remember what 'vocabulary sets' are? To help you remember, look back at Chapter 3.

Exercise 1
There are a lot of vocabulary sets in the text from the reading section. In groups of three, look at one sport each from the following sports: softball, karate and squash.

Try to find as many words in the text connected with this sport as possible. Make sure that you understand what the words mean. Use an English dictionary to help you. Then explain your words to the other two students.

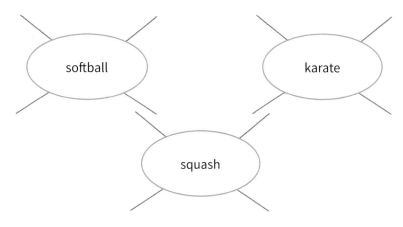

Exercise 2
Work in the same groups of three as in Exercise 1. Talk for about one minute about the sport that you chose, using as many of the words that you found in Exercise 1 as you can. Your teacher will time you.

🔊 Listening 1

Listening: activity 1
Before you listen, look at the list of sports below. In pairs, tell each other what you know about each sport. Then, listen to the three speakers in track 14 talking about a sport and try to match the sport to the correct speaker. There are more options than you need.

	Sports:
Speaker 1	Tennis
	Badminton
	Volleyball
Speaker 2	Basketball
	Golf
	Football
Speaker 3	Ice hockey

Listening: activity 2
Listen again and write down the words that helped you decide which sport each speaker was talking about. Then compare the list with your partner. Do you have the same words?

See Transcript 13 at the back of the book.

Study tip:
Using vocabulary sets in listening
In the vocabulary section we focused on different vocabulary sets (i.e. groups). Grouping related words together helps you guess a topic which may be unfamiliar and this skill is often tested in listening exercises.

Project

You are going to do some research into an unusual sport or activity. In your group choose one of the sports below. Research it together and write a short paragraph about it. If you can, bring in a picture of the sport, but don't show it to the other teams. Tell the other students about your sport. When you are reading out the information, don't mention the name of the sport. Other students will have to guess what sport you are talking about. In your description, try to use some phrases from the useful language section below.

> **Unusual sports:**
>
> | street luge | zorbing | curling | kite surfing |
> | --- | --- | --- | --- |
> | Sepak Takraw | underwater hockey | | |

Useful language:

- It features … teams / it is played by … (how many) players in … (where) with … (what)
- Its roots are set in … (country/continent)
- The competition is performed on/in … (where)
- … can use a variety of / a combination of allowed techniques such as …
- It involves …
- Each player/competitor must …
- … is/are not allowed
- It runs for a fixed time of …
- Points are awarded for … / A point is won when …
- Some of the world's current top-ranked … (players, competitors, champions) are … (names)

Discussion

After you have heard all the presentations, have a class discussion. Express your opinion (e.g. 'As for me …'), agree (e.g. 'You're absolutely right …') and disagree (e.g. 'I see what you mean, but …'). Also, ask other students what they think (e.g. 'Would you agree with that?').

- What do you think about the sports mentioned above?
- Which one is the craziest?
- Which one do you think is a fun activity rather than a competitive sport?
- Which one, in your opinion, is far too dangerous?
- Are any of these practised in your country?
- Which one would you like to try?

After hearing the presentations about sports, you have decided to join a local gym to take up a new sport (e.g. tennis). However, you want to find out more about the gym first. Write an email to a local gym enquiring about the following information.

- Their opening hours
- How much the membership fee is
- If they provide a personal trainer
- If you could have a trial session before you join

Listening 2

Pre-listening activity 1

How much do you know about the Olympic Games? In small groups answer the questions in the Olympic Games quiz. You'll get one point for each correct answer.

Olympic Games quiz

A Who was the main founder of the modern-day Olympic Games?

B Where did he come from?

C When were the first modern-day Olympic Games held?

D Where were the first Games held?

E Are the Winter and Summer Olympic Games held in the same year?

F How often are the Olympic Games held?

G Which cities have hosted the Summer or Winter Olympic Games more than once?

H These four cities are connected with the Summer Olympic Games. Can you put them in the correct chronological order? London; Athens; Rio de Janeiro; Beijing

I Where are the headquarters of the International Olympic Committee?

J Where is the Olympic torch lit?

93

Pre-listening activity 2

You are going to listen to a radio programme about the history of the Paralympics.

- What are the Paralympics?
- Do you know any famous Paralympians from your country or from other countries?
- Which sport do they compete in?

🎧 Vocabulary 3

The following words appear in the recording. Use an English dictionary to check the meaning of these words before you listen. For some of them, it might be helpful to look for a picture in a book or on the Internet to understand the meaning.

1 a wheelchair (noun)

2 a javelin (noun)

3 archery (noun)

4 annual (adjective)

5 a disability (noun)

6 to broadcast (verb)

7 a venue (noun)

Listening: activity 1

Look at the questions below about the Paralympics. Circle the important words in each question. Then listen to the radio programme in track 15 and choose the best option, A, B or C. You will hear the recording twice.

1 The first Stoke Mandeville Games were
   A   an international event
   B   held in London
   C   held in 1948.

2 What were the first sports at the Stoke Mandeville Games?
   A   wheelchair racing and discus throwing
   B   swimming and cycling
   C   javelin and archery

3 Why did Dr Guttmann want to organise these games?
   A   He wanted his patients to learn a new skill.
   B   He wanted to improve the quality of life of his patients.
   C   He wanted to introduce an annual event for his patients.

4 How many countries competed at the first Winter Paralympic Games?
   A   12
   B   14
   C   23

5 Before the Games were officially called the Paralympics, they grew in size because
   A   the number of categories increased
   B   a record number of 145 countries entered
   C   athletes with other disabilities were allowed to enter.

6 When were the Winter Paralympics first held at the same location as the Winter Olympics?
   A   1968
   B   1988
   C   1992

7 **What was special about the Paralympics in Atlanta?**
  A TV rights were sold for the first time.
  B A record number of people watched the Games on TV.
  C A record number of new sports were added to the Games.

8 **According to the speaker, competitors in the Paralympic Games are**
  A inspiring
  B successful
  C impressive.

See Transcript 14 at the back of the book.

> ### Key term: bare infinitive
>
> The infinitive verb form is generally written with 'to'. For example: *I want **to go** on holiday*. However, in some sentences we use the infinitive without 'to'. This is called the bare infinitive. For example: *I must **go** now*.

⊕ Language focus

Verb forms

Analysis

When we use two verbs together in English, the second verb takes one of these three forms:

A infinitive with 'to'

B bare infinitive

C *-ing* form.

Look at the examples from the listening about the Paralympics. Underline the second verb and decide which form this verb takes.

A He enjoyed watching them getting involved.

B … these didn't seem to have the same impact.

C He believed that sport could make his patients' lives much better.

Look at the following verbs. Which verb forms come after these verbs? With a partner, copy each heading into a box similar to below and put each verb in the correct box. If in doubt, use an English dictionary to help you.

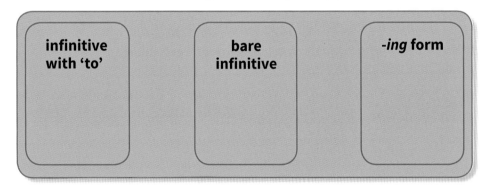

infinitive with 'to'	bare infinitive	*-ing* form

want	admit	should	make (somebody)	
can	deny	decide	must	finish
enjoy	suggest	offer	hope	ask (somebody)
deserve	would prefer	dislike		practise
intend	let (somebody)	keep		promise

95

Practice

Exercise 1
Read the following sentences and correct the mistakes.

1   Suki enjoys to go to the gym a lot.

2   Kelly let me to eat her sandwich.

3   Ivan has offered give his best friend all his DVDs.

4   Mohsin promised doing his English homework at the weekend.

5   Faran can running faster than any of his friends.

6   Tim asked me phone him tonight.

7   Ivan admitted to be often late for his swimming lessons.

8   I'd prefer going to the seaside this summer.

9   My brother suggested to go to the cinema tonight. What do you think?

10 Why don't you ask somebody help you with the project?

Exercise 2
Complete the sentences with your own ideas using the correct verb form.

1   I want …

2   I don't intend …

3   I promised …

4   My parents let me …

5   My parents make me …

6   A good friend should …

7   Everybody deserves …

8   I'd prefer …

Activate your English
In pairs, prepare a questionnaire for other students. Choose five verbs and make five correct questions.

For example:

want – What sport do you *want* to learn in the future?

Questionnaire

1

2

3

4

5

 Reading and writing

Pre-reading activity

In pairs, students ask each other at least one question using one of the words below.

For example, *'How often do you go to the gym?' 'Have you ever had a personal trainer?'*

(gym)   (gym equipment)   (personal trainer)   (workout)

Reading and writing: activity 1

You are going to read the personal profile of a girl called Christina who wants to join a local gym.

First, look at the form she has to fill in. Then read the text. Imagine you are Christina and complete the form with the correct information.

To help you remember how to do this exercise, look back at the rules in Chapter 4 about how to fill in a form.

Four years ago, Christina Aranda, who is from Colombia, was involved in an accident when she fell off her bike while she was cycling on a narrow path. It had been raining and the path, which is normally very safe, had become very muddy. Christina wasn't paying enough attention and went straight into the mud. The bike became stuck and she fell over the handlebars and landed hard on a rock. She broke her leg and cracked two of her ribs. She also twisted her wrist. Luckily, she had her mobile with her and could call the Accident and Emergency department at her local hospital on 041 6880203 for help. She also called her mum, Irene, to let her know what had happened. Her mum's number is 079 33391012.

She had to spend five days in hospital for tests and then she had to stay at home for a further two months. She also needed a lot of physiotherapy treatment after the fracture healed.

This happened when she was 16. Now Christina is 20 and her family has just moved to a new area in a town called Santa Marta, which is a port near Venezuela. Her new address is 14 El Prado Square, Santa Marta. She also got a new mobile for her birthday. Her new number is 076 77749399. Since the accident she has healed completely, but she still gets some pain occasionally so she needs to do gentle exercise to keep her body strong. Christina has always liked to keep fit. She used to go to a gym where her family lived before, but now she's looking for a new gym that is close to her new home.

Christina is very busy with her university assignments at the moment, so she would like to hire some of the equipment to take home with her. Some of the new gyms in town allow people to do that. It saves you time because you can do the exercise at home and it is much cheaper too.

Christina's plan is to get a personal trainer first. She would like to try out some new exercise machines such as treadmills and cross trainers, so she needs to know how to use them. She needs to be careful not to overdo the exercise because of her previous injuries so she plans to have a personal trainer for the first three lessons. A friend of hers was suggesting having a trainer for the first ten lessons, but Christina feels that ten lessons are unnecessary. Then, when she becomes more familiar with the equipment and her exercise routine, she would like to hire these two exercise machines to use at home for about three months. By then she will have finished her assignments and will have more time to go to the gym more regularly again.

The Tree of Life Gym
Application and Booking Form

Section A: Personal details

Full name: ....

Address: ....

....

....

Age: 16–18   19–25   26–35   36–45   over 45   (please circle)

Gender: Male/Female   (please delete)

Phone number (daytime): ....

Emergency contact name and number: ....

Section B: Requirements

Will you require a personal trainer?   ☐ Yes   ☐ No   (please tick)

For how many sessions would you like to book your personal trainer? ....

Would you like to hire any of the gym exercise equipment?

☐ Yes   ☐ No   (please tick)

What equipment will you require and for how long? Give details.

....

....

Section C

In the space below write **one sentence** stating why you would like to have a personal trainer or not, and **one sentence** giving details of any previous physical injuries we should know about.

....

....

....

....

....

....

Reading and writing: activity 2

When you have finished filling in the form, read your answers and check your spelling, punctuation, capital letters and grammar in Section C.

Compare your answers with your partner.

 Speaking and writing

Speaking and writing activity

Imagine you want to join the Tree of Life Gym. Think of the answers you would give. This doesn't have to be real information. You can invent the details. Do the role-play with a partner.

Student A: You want to join the gym. Phone the reception and give the receptionist the details you are asked for.

Student B: You work as a receptionist at the gym. Ask for the details required on the form and fill them in.

When you have finished, swap roles and repeat the activity.

Speaking activity

In groups discuss the following questions.

- How do you keep fit?
- Do you feel you do enough to keep fit or not? Why? Why not?
- Do you go to the gym? How often?
- What do you do at the gym? What equipment do you generally use?
- Do you do any group work-out activities? Give details.
- Would you like to have a personal trainer? Why? Why not?
- Do you prefer exercising outdoors or indoors? Why?
- Do you think your generation generally keeps fit or not? Give examples and reasons why or why not.
- What are the outcomes of not keeping fit in the long term, in your opinion?
- Why do you think there has been a big increase in obesity in recent years?
- What other benefits does exercising have apart from the physical ones?
- From your point of view, are people who live in the countryside healthier and fitter than people who live in a city? Why? Why not?

When you have finished your discussion, write a short paragraph about the outcomes of your discussion. Then present it to the class and compare the findings with other groups.

Useful language 1: presenting results/findings

- The vast majority of students believe that …
- The most common way of … is …
- 6 out of 15 students …
- Nearly half of the students …
- Only 30 per cent of people …
- Only a small minority of the students …
- Hardly anybody thinks that …

Useful language 2: comparing findings/ideas

- Our findings were identical to yours. We believe it is because …
- We have similar answers, but …
- Our opinions differ quite a lot from yours. We don't agree with the fact that …
- We have a completely different view on this topic. We feel that the main reason for … is …

Summary

Can you remember …

- at least **three** sports that are bidding for a place at the Olympic Summer Games in 2020?
- what the noun is from 'to include'?
- the words that mean: 'to be pulled by'; 'to originate / to come from'; 'to deal with a problem'?
- at least **three** words connected with badminton and ice hockey?
- at least **three** interesting facts about the Olympic Games?
- at least **four** interesting facts about the Paralympic Games?

- the **three** verb forms you learnt about in this chapter?
- at least **two** examples for each verb form?
- what is wrong with the two following sentences? 'My dad never lets stay out late.' 'Our teacher suggested to have a celebration at the end of the term.'
- **two** examples of exercise equipment?
- what a personal trainer is? Write down **two** advantages of having a personal trainer.

Progress check

Go back to the Objectives at the beginning of this chapter and assess your progress. Use the symbols below to show how confident you feel about your learning progress.

I am very good at this. ✓ ✓

I am OK, but I need a bit more practice. ✓

I can't do this yet and I need to look at this section again. ✗

Chapter 8:
Inventions

Objectives

In this chapter, you will learn and practise:
- reading skills – note-taking about inventions
- writing paper – writing a summary about: (a) misunderstood inventions and how successful they are now; (b) the advantages and disadvantages of the Internet
- speaking skills – discussing the topic of inventions, modern technology and the use of the Internet in everyday life
- listening skills – matching speakers to how they feel about an invention
- writing skills – writing an email to a friend about something you lost, and planning and organising your ideas before you start writing.

You will also learn and practise the following language skills:
- linkers of contradiction
- adjectives of attitudes and feelings
- '-ed/-ing' adjectives.

You will 'Activate your English' by:
- expressing advantages and disadvantages
- expressing attitudes and feelings.

Chapter 8: Inventions

📖 Reading and ✏️ writing

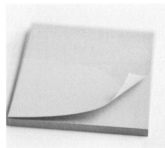

Pre-reading activity

In small groups discuss which inventions, in your opinion, are the most important ever invented.

In your groups, agree on a list of the top five inventions. Explain why you think they are essential in our lives.

Compare your list with other groups.

In the same groups, look at the pictures of inventions above. Did you have any of these in your top five list? Discuss the importance of these inventions.

- How did they change the way we live?
- How often do you use them?
- What would life be like without them?
- Have any of these inventions been developed into other things or are they still used in the same way?

❝ Vocabulary 1

Look at some words from the text about inventions. In two groups, look up the words in an English dictionary. Then explain the meanings to the students in the other group.

Group A

1 to take something for granted (phrase)

2 This wasn't always the case. (phrase)

3 to receive harsh criticism (adjective)

4 a novelty (noun)

5 This invention came about by accident. (phrasal verb)

6 an adhesive (noun)

Group B

1 to peel off something (verb)

2 The invention was shelved. (verb)

3 an obstacle (noun)

4 scrap paper (phrase)

5 remote (adjective)

6 sceptical (adjective)

Did you know?

The bagpipes, a typical Scottish instrument, were invented in Persia, not Scotland.

Reading: activity 1

Quickly scan the article about inventions that people didn't believe in and find the following numbers or names. What do they refer to? Explain these in your own words.

1 Spencer Silver
2 100
3 1.8 billion
4 2014
5 1876
6 Michael Aldrich
7 90 per cent
8 1960s
9 William Preece

And they said it would never work ...

Many inventions that we take for granted today faced a lot of criticism at the start from people who didn't believe in innovations, which they called strange, unnecessary and impractical.

The telephone

These days we all have at least one telephone at home and mobile phones have become such a vital part of our lives that we can't imagine going even one day without them. However, this wasn't always the case. After the invention of the telephone in 1876, it received harsh criticism from people like William Preece who was the leading engineer for the British Post Office at the time. He didn't feel that the telephone was needed, as the Post Office employed so-called messenger boys who did a good job delivering messages. Mr Preece thought the telephone was a novelty and, even though it may have been popular in America, that it wasn't going to become a hit in Britain. He couldn't have been more wrong. Telephones have now developed into mobile, smart and portable devices whose sales reached 1.8 billion units in 2013.

Sticky notes

This invention, commonly used in offices and households throughout the world, came about as a result of a series of accidents. In 1968 Spencer Silver, who was working for a company called 3M at the time, was trying to produce super-strong adhesive to be used in the building of planes. This, however, wasn't successful and instead he managed to create an extremely weak adhesive that was pressure-sensitive. The new adhesive had two advantages: it could be peeled off surfaces quite easily and it could be reused. In spite of these two positive features, nobody could see any practical use for it and, in the end, the invention was shelved.

A few years later, a product development engineer working for 3M, Art Fry, decided to use this adhesive for personal use. He stuck strips of paper in a book as page markers and a whole new concept was born. However, the idea still wasn't without obstacles. The challenge was to make the glue stay on the sticky note itself, rather than peeling off and staying on the surface it was attached to. Two more 3M employees were brought in and set the task of producing a coating for the adhesive so that it wouldn't detach itself and they managed just that. Unfortunately, 3M bosses still believed that this invention wasn't going to be commercially successful and people would continue to use scrap paper for their notes rather than sticky notes. That is why sticky notes were only trialled within the company, where they became extremely popular. It wasn't until many years later that 3M bosses finally decided to give out a vast amount of free samples to other companies to see if anyone would be interested in buying them. To their surprise, 90 per cent of the companies approached went on to order more sticky notes. This exceeded anybody's expectations. Nowadays, sticky notes come in a variety of shapes and colours and are sold in more than 100 countries.

Online shopping

Remote shopping was discussed long before online shopping was invented. In the 1960s, a lot of people were sceptical about remote shopping, their reason being that people preferred to see the products they were buying and to handle them in person before they decided to make a purchase. Another problem was the length of time it would take to deliver these products to the customer as the shipping speed was very slow.

Online shopping was piloted in the early 1980s. At that time it was called teleshopping, and although trading products remotely between businesses became possible within a year, shopping between businesses and customers didn't become commercially successful until the 1990s. Michael Aldrich, the father of online shopping, realised that the main obstacle to online shopping between businesses and customers was the inadequate telecommunication. It was clear to him that better telecommunication links to people's homes were needed. Of course nowadays with fast broadband this is not a problem any more.

We now buy almost everything online, from holidays to groceries. In fact in 2014, it was estimated that the industry would grow to $1.5 trillion globally.

Reading: activity 2

Your school has dedicated this week to technology and inventions. You have decided to give a talk to other students about inventions which are widely used today, but were badly received by people in the past. You will need to make notes for your talk. Read the text about inventions and make your notes under each heading.

To help you, the relevant information has been highlighted for you in the article.

Reasons why some people thought these inventions wouldn't work.

* ....
* ....
* ....

Practical difficulties with some of the inventions.

* ....
* ....

Examples to show evidence that the inventions are now successful.

* ....
* ....

Reading and writing: activity 1

Your talk has been a success with the other students and you have decided to write a short summary for the school magazine. Look at your notes again. Using the ideas, write about how misunderstood the inventions were and how successful they are now.

Your summary should be about 70 words long (and no more than 80 words long). You should use your own words as far as possible.

Before you start writing, look back at Chapter 5 and the Study tip box about writing a summary. Then write your answer.

To help you, part of the summary has already been written. Can you add the missing ideas and make them fit the gaps?

Not all inventions used today were successful right from the start. For example, people thought that ....

....

because ....

However, today this invention is very successful. It is ....

....

which proves that the critics were wrong in the first place.

(37 words used, 33 words left for you to use)

Pre-reading activity

You are going to read about the Internet. Work in two groups.

- Group A: try to think of the advantages of the Internet.
- Group B: try to think of the disadvantages of the Internet.

Reading and writing: activity 2

You are going to give a short talk to your class about the advantages and disadvantages of the Internet. Read the following article about the Internet and prepare some notes to use as the basis for your talk.

Make your notes under each heading.

The advantages of using the Internet:

- ....
- ....
- ....
- ....

The disadvantages of using the Internet:

- ....
- ....
- ....

The invention we can't live without

A lot has been written about the most useful inventions, from the electric light bulb to antibiotics. However, we have now entered the age of high technology and even though all these inventions are extremely important in different ways, one of them stands head and shoulders above all the others. It was invented in the 1960s, and it was first intended for sharing information in scientific and military fields. Over the years, it has developed to become the powerful tool we know and use every day. It is, of course, the Internet.

It is still mainly used for its original purpose – searching for and sharing information, not only by professionals, but also by individuals for private use. Time is money nowadays, so it is essential to locate information quickly. Research for an assignment, for example, is much easier from the comfort of your own home. Long hours spent at the library are now a thing of the past, because everything you need is at your fingertips. This, however, brings some drawbacks. Finding a book from a reputable source used to be almost guaranteed at the library. If you were in doubt, the librarian would help and advise you on recommended authors. These days the information on the Internet can be uploaded by any member of the public. This poses the problem of whether the information you are using in your project is accurate or reliable.

Nevertheless, we don't use the Internet only as an information source. The world has been brought closer together than ever before because of the increase in the number of ways we can communicate. Keeping in touch with your relatives on the other side of the world couldn't be easier. Many of us send an email every day, use Skype to talk to our loved ones, or share holiday pictures with friends on Facebook. The list is endless. Communication is not just with somebody we know. People are keen to share their views on Twitter with the public or write about their experiences in their own blogs, which have replaced the old-fashioned diary. Smartphones have enabled us to record anything, anywhere and at any time, and these videos can immediately be posted on YouTube for others to see. This, sadly, has caused us to lose our privacy. The Internet can also contribute to the loss of career prospects. How many times have we heard about job applicants being rejected because inappropriate pictures, videos or tweets have been made public?

The Internet has spared us all the trouble of going to the bank, supermarkets, music shops or colleges. Shopping online, for example, couldn't be easier. If we need a present for a friend quickly, we can go to our favourite shopping website, see some reviews of the product we have chosen, select and click. A few days later, you have the present in the comfort of your home. This all sounds very good, but what impact has online shopping had on the shops in your local area? A number of shops have found it impossible to compete with the hassle-free shopping which is offered online and have had to take the drastic measure of closing down. Is this the end of an era? Will all shopping be done online? How will the future of banks, cinemas and schools be affected?

As all aspects of our lives have become intertwined with the Internet, this has, unfortunately, brought new problems and risks. Identity theft was almost unheard of 20 years ago. Nowadays, due to people's poor judgement of how much information to share over the Internet, identity theft is a common occurrence. Also, when you hear somebody speaking about a virus, you can guarantee that they are not looking for medical help, but for an IT specialist.

Good or bad, the Internet has penetrated all parts of our life, and without it life would simply be unthinkable.

🎧 Vocabulary 2

Exercise 1

Elsewhere in this book you have discussed how important it is to guess unknown words from the context when you are reading. Look at the highlighted words and phrases in the article about the Internet and try to guess what they mean. Then compare your ideas with your partner's ideas.

Exercise 2
Now look at the definitions below and match the highlighted words and phrases in the text to their correct definitions.

1   very long

2   very easy, without problems

3   is noticeably better than the rest

4   happens very often, is not unusual to see

5   disadvantages, the downside

6   want to do it very much

7   closely connected with something

8   very convenient, very near and ready to be used

9   to do something extreme and unwanted, but necessary

Reading and writing: activity 3

Imagine you have given your talk about the Internet to the class. Your teacher has asked you to write a short summary for students who were absent.

Look at your notes in activity 2. Using the ideas in your notes, write a short summary about the advantages and disadvantages of the Internet.

Your summary should be about 70 words long (and no more than 80 words long). You should use your own words as far as possible.

◯ Speaking

In small groups discuss the following points.

- What is your favourite invention of all time?
- How has this invention changed our lives?
- Can you think of any useless inventions? Why do you find them useless?
- Are there any inventions that are too dangerous for humankind and should never have been invented? Give examples.
- How important is the Internet in your life?
- What do you use it for?
- Do you think that very young children should be allowed to use the Internet unsupervised? Why? Why not?
- We use the Internet for banking, downloading music and films, and shopping. In your view, will shops, cinemas and banks disappear in the near future?
- How do you feel about online courses and learning? Would you ever try a course like this? Give reasons for or against.
- Do you think that schools will disappear in the future? Why? Why not?
- Is technology always helpful?
- Do you think that with more technology, such as the Internet, being used in everyday life, we are losing our privacy? Give examples.

Project

There are countries that have given us very important inventions. For example, China has given us paper. Do some group research on other famous inventions.

- Who invented these inventions?
- Where do they come from?
- How have they changed people's lives?

Then prepare a short talk for the rest of the class.

Can you name an invention from your country? Apart from inventions, can you name other things that come from your country and are well known all over the world? For example, food, music, dance, etc. Have a class discussion.

Imagine that you have bought a product online that is completely new to the market. When you received it, you weren't very happy with it. Write an email to complain about the product.

In your email remember to mention the following:

- what you bought, from which website and when you bought it
- what is wrong with the product OR other things you weren't happy about
- what you want the company to do about it (e.g. refund your money, replace it, etc.).

Language focus

Linkers of contradiction

Analysis

Look at some sentences about the Internet and circle the linkers. What two ideas do they link together?

A Even though all these inventions are extremely important, not many people know about them.

B Research for an assignment is much easier from your own home. However, you often get distracted.

C The Internet is very useful for finding information. Nevertheless, sometimes the information is not accurate.

There are more linkers of contradiction in the reading text, 'And they said it would never work …'. Look through the text and find more examples of these linkers. Notice how the linkers are used. Now use them to rewrite the two sentences below as one sentence. Use an English dictionary to help you.

I had a terrible headache.

I helped my friend with his homework.

How do we use the linkers?

- Do we need to use commas?
- Do we have to start a new sentence when we use them?
- Are they followed by a noun or a sentence (i.e. a subject with a verb)?

Key term: contradiction

We talk about contradiction when we use two opposing ideas together.

For example, *The tablet was really expensive.* **However,** *I bought it.*

The first sentence tells us something negative (i.e. 'expensive'), so we imagine that the person would not buy it. The second sentence has introduced an idea that we don't expect – 'I bought it'. These two ideas contradict each other.

Practice

Exercise 1

Rewrite the two sentences using the linker in the brackets.

1   It was raining. I went for a jog. (despite)

2   I was angry with her. I smiled. (although)

3   The test was hard. I passed with top marks. (however)

4   Rodrigo was tired. He joined us for a walk. (but)

5   Marta has a lot of clothes. She keeps buying more. (in spite of)

6   I can't cook. I agreed to cook lunch for my best friend. (nevertheless)

7   It was very late at night. I phoned Gaby for help. (even though)

8   I wasn't feeling well. I went to school. (despite)

Exercise 2

There are some mistakes in the following sentences. With a partner, find them and correct them.

1   In spite of it was late, I wasn't feeling tired.

2   He'd been studying very hard. Nonetheless he failed the exam.

3   She had very little experience although she was offered the job.

4   Even though I don't like romantic comedies I'm going to see one with Nadia tomorrow.

5   Despite of the noise coming from the street, I fell asleep.

6   I normally go to the cinema at the weekend however this weekend I'm going to the museum of unusual inventions.

Activate your English

In groups, discuss the advantages and disadvantages of the following inventions. Use a wide range of contradiction linkers. You can also use linkers of addition (e.g. *and, moreover, furthermore*) if you are listing more than one advantage or more than one disadvantage.

mobile phone	television	e-books

wind farms	cars	credit cards

Listening

Pre-listening activity

Look at the following inventions. What are they used for? Do you have one? How often do you use it/them? Could you live without them?

- a vacuum cleaner
- an MP3 player
- contact lenses
- a laptop
- a microwave
- a mobile phone
- an e-book

Listening: activity 1

Listen to six speakers in track 16 talking about an invention. Which invention from the list above are they talking about? Match each invention to the correct speaker. There is one extra invention that you don't need to use.

With a partner, discuss the words that you heard which helped you to decide on your answers.

Listening: activity 2

Listen again to the six recordings. Each speaker expresses their feelings about the inventions. Choose from the list A–G and write the letter next to the correct speaker. Use each letter only once. There is one extra letter which you do not need to use.

Speaker 1:	**A** I'm scared of using it.
Speaker 2:	**B** I felt frustrated.
Speaker 3:	**C** I was satisfied.
Speaker 4:	**D** I was excited.
Speaker 5:	**E** I find it impractical.
Speaker 6:	**F** I find this invention difficult to use.
	G I was disappointed.

See Transcript 15 at the back of the book.

 **Vocabulary 3**

Attitudes and feelings

Exercise 1

In the listening exercise, people expressed their feelings about some inventions. Look at Transcript 15 and find words or phrases that match the following phrases.

Speaker 1:
- I didn't expect that.
- I was angry.
- I was discouraged.

Study tip:
Matching speakers, lexical links and implied information

In this type of listening exercise, you are asked to match speakers to, for example, their opinions, feelings or intentions.

Learning different phrases that express these opinions, feelings or intentions will be helpful.

For example, when the speaker says: 'It was a real **let-down**,' you know that the speaker was **disappointed**.

However, sometimes the speaker may only imply their opinion, feeling or intention.

For example, when the speaker is asked: **'Are you tired?'** and the answer is: **'Well, I think I'd like to go home actually.'** We don't get a direct answer, but we know that the speaker is tired. They implied they want to go home, so we know they're probably feeling tired.

Speaker 2:
- I was happy.
- I was disappointed.

Speaker 3:
- I was very happy.

Speaker 4:
- I was satisfied.

Speaker 6:
- I find it difficult.
- I don't find it easy.

Exercise 2

Look at these four adjectives and try to think of more words or phrases that have a similar meaning. Then use a thesaurus dictionary to check. Did you find some which have a stronger meaning?

happy	unhappy	angry	difficult

Some adjectives can take the suffix *-ed* or *-ing*. Look at the two sentences. What is the difference in meaning?

A   I'm really very **interested** in the lives of some inventors.

B   The lives of some inventors are really **interesting**.

Which suffix do we use to talk about somebody's feelings?

Which suffix do we use to describe a situation, person, place or thing?

Exercise 3

Complete the sentences using the correct suffix (i.e. *-ed/-ied*, or *-ing/-ying*).

1   I found the new James Bond film really bor....... .

2   I was really fascinat......... by the museum of unusual inventions. Can we go again?

3   She was discourag......... by the way they spoke to her in that shop.

4   I'm sure you'll love the new album. It's very original and the music on it is really relax......... .

5   That was the most embarrass........... moment of my life when my mobile went off in the middle of the lesson.

6   Everyone looked shock........ by the news about the head teacher leaving the school.

7   From what you are saying the new library in Birmingham must be really fascinat.......... . I think it was designed by a Dutch architect.

8   You must be feeling really disappoint........... . You put so much effort into the design and then it didn't get selected.

9 That was such a satisf............. story. I didn't expect it to be so good.

10 Have you just seen a ghost? You look really terrif............ .

Activate your English
In pairs tell each other about the following.

- The most interesting book you've ever read.
- The most boring film you've ever seen.
- When you feel excited.
- When you last felt cross and why.
- What you find tricky and why.

Now choose one of the following topics and talk about it to the class for about one minute. Don't mention the key words in the topic (e.g. 'struggle'). Try to use synonyms instead. Other students must guess which topic you are talking about.

> **a real let-down**   **an embarrassing moment**   **something that puts me off**
>
> **something I struggle with**   **a thrilling experience**   **surprising news**

 Writing

Pre-writing activity
Have you ever lost anything? What was it? Where did you lose it? How did you feel about it? Did you find it?

Writing: activity 1
Read this exam-type question. Then think of some ideas with a partner and make a few notes.

Imagine you have lost something that you use every day and that you can't live without. You were so upset that you decided to write an email to a friend about it. In your email you should:

- say what you lost and where you lost it
- describe what you were doing when you lost it
- explain what you have learnt from the experience.

Your email should be between 100 and 150 words long. Do not write an address.

The picture may give you some ideas and you should try to use some ideas of your own.

Writing: activity 2
- What do you do before you start writing?
- How do you record the ideas you want to use in your writing?
- Look at the following students' ideas on the next page. How did the students organise their ideas? Which way do you like the best? Which one is the easiest to follow and the most useful for you?

Student A

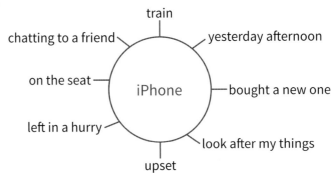

Student B
laptop – McDonald's
lunch – tired – forgot
home – cried – never again laptop outside

Student C
- very important to me
- school library
- doing my homework
- thinking about a lot of things
- MP3 player
- next to the computer

Writing: activity 3
Use your notes from the planning stage in activity 1 and write your answer. Don't forget to read your answer carefully and check it for mistakes.

Writing: activity 4
Read the sample answer to the exam-type question. What are the student's answers to the questions in the bullet points in activity 1? Are the ideas well organised?

● ○ ○ New Message

To : _____ From : _____

Hi Xia,

You'll never believe this, but I lost my precious MP3 player that I got for my last birthday. I was so upset I couldn't sleep that night. I was really cross with myself for not being careful enough. I realised how careless I am with my things and also how much I love my music. I can't be without listening to music for more than a day.

Anyway, how are you doing? How are you getting on with the exam revision? I'm really snowed under with schoolwork myself and that's why I need my MP3 player when I go out jogging. It relaxes me. That reminds me, do you want to join me next time? Plus, I wanted to ask you if you fancy coming to the cinema with me. Let me know.

Oh, I haven't told you yet, but I lost it on the bus. I had it in my hand and then I put it on the seat next to me because Suzie phoned me. We were chatting and I got off the bus without it.

All the best,

Min-Hui

Did you know?

Most lost items found on the London Underground are found on the Piccadilly Line, which goes to Heathrow Airport. Lost items have included false teeth and a wedding dress bought in Peru.

Writing: activity 5

Look at the email in activity 4 again. How would you organise the ideas into paragraphs?

Paragraph 1:

Paragraph 2:

Paragraph 3:

Writing: activity 6

Choose one of the ways to organise ideas from activity 2 and write another email. Organise your ideas into logical paragraphs. Try to use some of the phrases and linkers that have been highlighted in the sample email by Min-Hui.

Summary

Can you remember …

- the words that mean: a) to decide not to use something right now, but maybe later, b) paper used for notes, c) a problem that stops you from being successful?
- **three** inventions that were predicted to be unsuccessful, but became very popular?
- the reason why the telephone was predicted to be a failure?
- what the missing words are from the following phrases? 'to stand ……… and shoulders above all the rest'; 'to have everything at your ……………'; 'to take drastic ……………'?
- what the phrases above mean?
- **one** linker of contradiction that is followed by a noun, **one** that is followed by a subject and a verb, and **one** that needs a comma?

- what the mistake is in the following sentence? 'Despite of it was raining, we decided to go jogging.'
- how to use 'in spite of', 'although' and 'however'? Think of three contrasting ideas for the use of mobile phones or computers and make three sentences using these linkers.
- **three** synonyms for 'happy' and **two** for 'angry'?
- when we use the suffix -ed and when we use -ing with adjectives?
- if the following suffixes are used correctly? 'I was really boring with the book. It wasn't particularly interesting.'
- what to do before you start writing?
- when we use 'you'll never believe this' and 'that's why'? Make **two** sentences using these expressions.

Progress check

Go back to the Objectives at the beginning of this chapter and assess your progress. Use the symbols below to show how confident you feel about your learning progress.

I am very good at this. ✓ ✓

I am OK, but I need a bit more practice. ✓

I can't do this yet and I need to look at this section again. ✗

Chapter 9:
Endangered species

Objectives

In this chapter, you will learn and practise:
- reading skills – answering questions about endangered tigers
- speaking skills – discussing the topic of animals
- listening skills – completing sentences about endangered species
- writing skills – writing an article about keeping animals in zoos, planning a piece of writing and paragraphing.

You will also learn and practise the following language skills:
- phrases to ask for clarification and to say 'I don't know'
- present perfect simple, present perfect continuous.

You will 'Activate your English' by:
- talking about life experience.

Chapter 9: Endangered species

📖 Reading

Pre-reading activity

Look at these pictures of some endangered animal species. With a partner, answer the questions.

1 Can you name the animals?
2 What do you know about these animals?
3 Can you find them in your country?
4 Do you know any endangered animals that live in your country?

Reading: activity 1

You are going to read an article about tigers and their critical situation. Scan the first paragraph. There are four numbers. What do the numbers refer to?

1 30   **3** 3200

2 5000–7500   **4** 100 000

🔖 Vocabulary 1

Before you read the article and answer some questions, look at some of the highlighted words in the text. Can you guess their meaning? Here are some clues to help you.

Paragraph 1:

become extinct – Look at the table. Can you see all the subspecies of tigers nowadays? Why? Why not?

captivity – Why is 'in the wild' mentioned in the same sentence?

diminishing – Look at the numbers mentioned in previous sentences. Why are they mentioned?

CAN THEY SURVIVE?

Although the tiger is one of the most powerful mammals, it is also at the greatest risk of becoming extinct. In fact, as many as three subspecies of tigers have become extinct in the last 30 years and there is a danger of this happening to even more of the subspecies. Recent estimates put the population of all tigers (including the ones in captivity) at around 5000–7500, with only about 3200 in the wild. At the beginning of the 20th century, this number was closer to about 100 000. This shows how fast the population of tigers is diminishing, and if care is not taken, this majestic mammal will soon be extinct.

In 2013 there were six subspecies of tigers in existence and all of them were classified as endangered.

Subspecies	Status	Number alive
Bengal Tiger	Endangered	Around 2000
Indochinese Tiger	Endangered	Around 1200
Malayan Tiger	Endangered	Around 800
Amur Tiger	Endangered	Around 600
Sumatran Tiger	Endangered	Around 500
South China Tiger	Endangered	Fewer than 50
Caspian Tiger	Extinct	Last seen approx. 1970s
Bali Tiger	Extinct	Last seen approx. 1930s
Javan Tiger	Extinct	Last seen approx. 1980s

There are very few tigers left in the world today and if adequate care is not taken, even these will be wiped out from the face of the Earth. The South China Tiger, for example, is nearly extinct, with less than 50 remaining today. With so few living in the wild, it has been at least 20 years since a South China Tiger was last spotted, and many people believe that this subspecies is already extinct.

In ancient times, tiger hunting was a popular sport among royalty. Some people also kept tigers as pets. In some countries, a number of superstitions exist regarding tigers. For example, an object made out of a tiger's claw is considered to have supernatural powers.

In more recent times, tigers have been hunted for their fur. Their body organs have also been rumoured to be a cure for many human medical conditions. This has resulted in the reckless poaching of tigers, making them an endangered species today.

Humans have also changed the natural habitat of the tiger. In many areas their habitat has been destroyed by cutting down trees and polluting the atmosphere. Furthermore, humans have hunted their prey, forcing tigers to either starve or take more risks.

The tiger does not hunt any animal larger than itself, such as the elephant, but relies on catching smaller animals for food. Tigers are also very good climbers and swimmers. This ability to adapt saves them from natural disasters and floods.

Serious action is now being taken to help the survival of this beautiful animal which is very close to extinction. All subspecies of the tiger are considered endangered and the hunting or poaching of them is illegal all over the world. China has banned the sale of all tiger-related products since 1993. Since then, however, illegal poaching for their fur has become more widespread.

The charity WWF is attempting to stop the decline of the tiger and to increase their numbers, both in the wild and in captivity. The goal of the WWF is to double the number of tigers in the world by 2022, which will be the Year of the Tiger according to the Chinese calender. There are other organisations that are also taking steps to prevent the extinction of this animal. We can only hope that all the efforts taken will prove to be successful.

www.buzzle.com/articles/endangered-tigers.html

Reading: activity 2

Read the following questions and highlight the key words. Then read the whole text to find the answers.

1   What do all six surviving subspecies of tigers have in common?

2   According to the table, which two types of tigers are the most endangered?

3   When was the South China Tiger last seen?

4   Why were tigers hunted by royalty in the distant past?

5   What part of a tiger is believed to have special powers?

6   According to the article, what other part of a tiger's body is thought to have healing powers?

7   How did people damage the tiger's natural environment? Give **two** details.

8   According to the writer, why are tigers likely to survive natural disasters? Give **two** examples.

9   What has been illegal since 1993?

10 What is the charity WWF trying to achieve by the Year of the Tiger?

Reading: activity 3

The reading text 'Can they survive?' contains a table with information about different subspecies of tiger. Look at the table again and write three questions for your partner to answer. Then swap your questions and find the answers in the table.

For example: Which subspecies has not been seen since the 1930s?

Reading: activity 4

In chapter 6 you learnt about different graphs and charts. Look back at the Study tip to remind yourself. Then look at the graph and chart below and answer the questions.

1   According to the graph, which of the animals live the longest?

2   How long can swans live?

3   Which animals have a shorter life than the Galapagos tortoise?

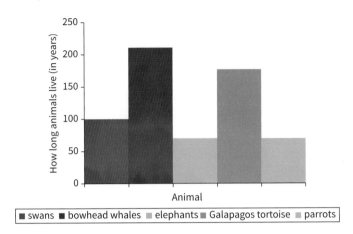

Data taken from: http://www.sciencemuseum.org.uk/onlinestuff /snot/whats_the_oldest-living_
animal_and_how_old_does_it_get.aspx

4   According to the pie chart, which was the second most popular pet in the UK
     in 2013?

5   Which pet was less popular than rabbits the UK in 2013?

Popular pets in the UK in 2013

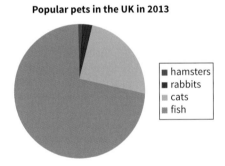

Data taken from: http://www.pfma.org.uk/pet-population/

Did you know?

• Bengal tigers are the most
  common type of tigers in
  the world.

• A tiger can eat up to 27 kg
  of meat in one night when
  very hungry. Tigers are
  nocturnal hunters.

• You won't find two tigers
  with identical stripes.

🗨 Speaking

In small groups answer the following questions. Then compare your answers
with the other groups.

1   What is your favourite animal?

2   Why do you like this animal?

3   Do people in your country keep a lot of pets?

4   What is the most popular pet in your country?

5   Why do you think people keep pets?

6   Do you think people always treat animals well? Give examples.

7   What did people use animals for in the past?

8   Do we still use animals in the same way nowadays? Why? Why not?

9   Why do you think we should save endangered species? Give reasons.

10   Do you feel too little / too much money is spent on trying to save endangered
     animals?

Project

You are going to research some endangered animals. Look at the photos at the start of the Reading section. In small groups, choose one of the animals and research it in more detail. Cover the following points:

- name of the animal
- the country of its origin
- its natural habitat
- interesting facts about the life of the animal
- the numbers of them remaining
- why it is endangered
- what animal conservation projects there are
- whether the projects have been successful
- what the future predictions are for this animal.

After you have collected your information, prepare your talk.

When you are listening to other groups' talks, take some notes. Which of the animals is in the greatest danger?

Now use your notes and the information from all the talks to write a report about conservation projects. These can be from your country, or from around the world. In your report remember to mention the following:

- what the project focuses on
- who is involved
- what is being done to improve the situation
- how the situation has changed since the project started
- your personal recommendations – what else could be done.

🗨 Speaking and 🔊 listening

Listening: activity 1

Sometimes when you are having a discussion, you may not understand what another person is trying to say, or you don't know how to answer their question. There are phrases that we use in conversation to let the other person know that they need to repeat or explain more.

Listen to four short dialogues between two students in track 17. What happens to the second student in each case? Match the situations A–D to the correct speaker. Then listen again and write down the phrase that the second student uses in each case.

Speaker 1:	**A** The student can't think of any examples.
Speaker 2:	**B** The student is trying to avoid the topic.
Speaker 3:	**C** The student can't answer the question at the moment.
Speaker 4:	**D** The student doesn't understand what has been said.

See Transcript 16 at the back of the book.

Study tip:
Asking for clarification

When you are speaking to somebody and don't understand what they are saying, you should ask them for clarification. This will help the conversation to continue. If you don't ask, the conversation may break down.

For example, you can say: 'I'm afraid I'm not following.'

Listening: activity 2

Look at a few more phrases. Can you match them to the correct statement in Listening activity 1?

1 Sorry, I'm not following.
2 Sorry, I didn't quite catch that.
3 It's too early to say.
4 Sorry, how do you mean?
5 Sorry, my mind's gone completely blank.

Pronunciation

Listen to the five phrases in Listening activity 2 (track 18) and mark the word that is stressed in each phrase. Then listen again and repeat.

See Transcript 17 at the back of the book.

Speaking

In pairs make short dialogues based on the situations below. When you are talking together try to use one of the phrases from Listening activities 1 and 2.

Situation 1: Invite each other to a party. Give directions how to get there.

Situation 2: Talk to each other about what your plans are for the next academic year.

Situation 3: Ask each other how much you know about endangered animals in your country.

Situation 4: Ask each other what makes you happy and sad.

Language focus

Present perfect simple and continuous

Analysis

Look at the sentences, some of which are taken from the Reading section. All the sentences contain verbs in the present perfect. Can you underline the present perfect simple and circle the present perfect continuous?

Key term: state and action verbs

State verbs (e.g. *believe, own, love*) can't be used in continuous forms (e.g. present continuous). This means you can only use them in the simple form (e.g. present simple).

For example, I *like your new dress.* **CORRECT**

~~I'm liking~~ *your new dress.* **WRONG**

Action verbs (e.g. *run, write, eat*) can be used in both forms: simple or continuous.

For example, *I always cook for my younger sister OR I'm cooking Mexican food today.* **BOTH ARE CORRECT**

1 Three subspecies of tigers have become extinct in the last 30 years.

2 The number of surviving tigers has been declining dramatically for the past few years.

3 This has also resulted in the reckless poaching of tigers.

4 Humans have also changed the natural habitat of the tiger.

5 Some countries have been trying to save the remaining tigers for many years now.

6 I've never seen a tiger in its natural environment, but I've seen them many times in the zoo.

7 I've always liked tigers. They're very graceful animals.

With a partner try to answer the following questions. Underline the correct answer.

1 Which tense is used for actions still in progress?
present perfect simple / present perfect continuous

2 Which tense is used for a completed action?
present perfect simple / present perfect continuous

3 Which tense is used to show a change from past to present?
present perfect simple / present perfect continuous

4 Which tense is used to talk about our experiences?
present perfect simple / present perfect continuous

5 Which tense is commonly used with time expressions such as 'for many years', 'for the past few years', etc? *present perfect simple / present perfect continuous*

6 Which tense is commonly used with expressions of frequency such as 'once', 'many times', 'never', etc? *present perfect simple / present perfect continuous*

7 Which tense is used with state verbs such as 'like'?
present perfect simple / present perfect continuous

State verbs
The verb 'like' is a state verb. This means it can only be used in simple tenses. Look at the following verbs and circle all the state verbs.

know	run	belong	read	love	study	hate	watch
	believe	eat	own	want	work	listen	

Study tip:
Using the dictionary for grammar – verbs
When you learn a new verb, check in a dictionary to see if the verb:

- is a **state verb** or an **action verb**
- is **regular** or **irregular**
- needs an **object**, or **not**.
  For example, the verb 'look' doesn't need an object. You can say: 'Look!' However, the verb 'tell' needs an object. You have to say: 'Tell <u>me</u> the truth.'

This information will help you when you want to use the new verb accurately in your speaking or writing.

Practice

Exercise 1
Look at the following sentences. Which tense do you need: present perfect simple or present perfect continuous?

1 I ...... (know) my best friend since we were little kids.

2 I ...... (study) English at this school for six years and I still have two more to do.

3 Tim ...... (listen) to music since he got up this morning.

4 My sister ...... (always want) to work with animals ever since she was a little girl.

5 I ...... (never like) winter. It's too cold and there's nothing to do outside.

6   You ...... (run) up and down the street for 30 minutes. Don't you think it's time you stopped?

7   How long ...... you ...... (read) this book?

8   How many times ...... you ...... (read) this book?

9   How long ...... you ...... (have) this bike? It looks very new.

10 Your hair looks nice. ...... you ...... (have) a haircut?

11 I ...... (buy) a new pair of trainers. Do you like them?

12 They ...... (come) to see us once. That was last month and I ...... (not see) them since then.

13 We'd better wake him up. He ...... (sleep) for 12 hours now.

14 I'm sorry I think I ...... (oversleep). It won't happen again.

Exercise 2

Complete the sentences below with your own ideas and then tell your partner.

1   I've always wanted to …

2   I've never believed that …

3   I've been … for ages.

4   I've only … once.

5   I've known …

6   I've … since …

7   My parents have never … in my entire life.

8   I've just …

9   I've always thought that …

10 For the past 10 minutes I've …

Activate your English

Think for a few minutes about your life and what you have already done in your life. Think about how long you've been doing certain things or how many times you have done them. You can choose from the following list.

- a course / learning new things
- exams
- a possession
- friends
- interesting experiences (e.g. travelling)
- a project you're working on
- moving house
- sports and games
- pets
- recent changes

Look at the diagram and make short notes in the shapes provided. Then tell your partner about your life.

Your partner can ask you additional questions like: 'How long have you …?', 'How many times have you …?', 'Have you ever …?' or 'When did you …?'

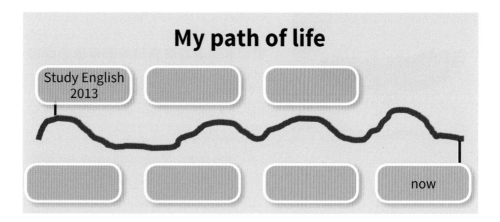

My path of life

Study English 2013

now

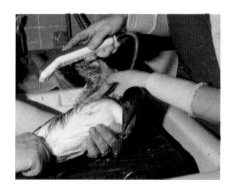  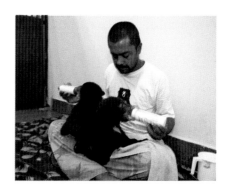

🔊 Listening

Pre-listening activity

You are going to listen to a talk about endangered animals and how we try to save them. First, with a partner, discuss the following questions.

- Do you know any endangered animals that live in your country?
- What is being done to save them?
- Do you know about any other conservation projects round the world?

The pictures above may give you some ideas.

❝ Vocabulary 2

Here are some words from the Listening section. Before you listen, check that you understand their meaning. Use an English dictionary to look up their meaning.

- to make an effort (phrase)
- vulnerable (adjective)
- predictions (noun)
- fatal (adjective)
- to work relentlessly (adverb)
- a haven for (noun)
- to breed (verb)

Listening: activity 1

In track 19, you will hear a talk given by a man about endangered animals and the efforts to save them. Read the notes and try to predict the type of answers you will need. Then listen to the talk and complete the sentences below. Write one or two words only for each gap.

You will hear the talk twice.

Endangered species

A Endangered animals are placed into categories according to their existing ....

B The group of animals considered at the lowest level of risk in the wild are described as ....

C If no serious action is taken .... of the animals that are at risk now will disappear in the future.

Reasons for species becoming endangered

D .... is one example of how people can harm the animals' habitat.

E The introduction of a species that is new to the area frequently leads to .... results for the existing species as they can't compete.

Saving endangered animals

F Lately, thanks to the involvement of .... , the issue of endangered species has been promoted more widely.

G Some villages in India have been asked to .... to provide a safe place for tigers to live.

H The numbers of eagles in some areas were monitored by ....

See Transcript 18 at the back of the book.

Listening: activity 2

When you are tested on listening, you are often tested on listening for numbers.

Listen to the talk again and write down all the numbers you hear. What do they refer to?

When you have finished, compare your answers with your partner. Do you agree?

Listening: activity 3

In pairs, practise saying the numbers from activity 2.

Now write down examples of the following numbers.

- a percentage
- a year
- a number with six figures
- a telephone number
- a time
- a date

Read your examples to your partner. Your partner must listen and write down the exact number. At the end check their answers. Are they the same as your numbers?

 Reading and writing

Pre-reading activity

You are going to read an article about whether zoos are a good or bad idea. What do you think? Are you for or against the idea of zoos, and why?

In pairs, discuss this question.

Reading: activity 1

Can you remember which paragraph gives you the overall opinion of the writer?

Which of the following sentences best summarises the ideas in that paragraph?

Find the correct paragraph and choose the best summary below.

A   Zoos are a bad idea because animals are not treated well.

B   Zoos are a good idea because they help to increase the number of endangered animals.

C   Zoos are doing a good job keeping endangered species, but there still needs to be a lot of improvement.

66 Vocabulary 3

Before you read the article again for more detail, look at the words/phrases below and match them to the highlighted words in the text. Only do the words/phrases from one of the lists (student A or student B). When you have finished, explain the new words to your partner.

Student A
Paragraphs 1 and 2

1   every day (phrase)

2   intentions (noun)

3   not moving (phrase)

4   to cause pressure (phrase)

5   to cause a public disagreement (phrase)

6   to move from one place to another with no purpose (verb)

7   to be forced to stay in a small area (phrase)

Student B
Paragraphs 3, 4 and 5

1   the green parts of a plant (noun)

2   it's very likely (phrase)

3   to be without an end (adverb)

4   public supporters (nouns)

5   becoming smaller until very little, or nothing, is left (verb)

6   when someone is left permanently by their parent (noun)

7   without a doubt (adverb)

ARE ZOOS BAD FOR ANIMALS?

Zoos have existed since ancient times and were features of the great courts of Egypt and China. The display of exotic animals was, for a long time, a show of wealth and power. Today, zoos focus on the conservation of animal species and the education of the public. Yet critics suggest that animals should not be kept in confinement.

Some animals are distinctly unsuited for life in a zoo, however noble the aims of the organisation. Keeping elephants in captivity has long sparked controversy among animal rights activists. Elephants in the wild roam constantly, covering a wide territory on a daily basis. In captivity, they have no choice but to stand still for long periods of time and this puts severe strain on the legs and feet of these giants, leading to chronic injury in some captive animals.

Yet elephants are a threatened species in their native environments and are heavily poached for ivory, leather and meat. In order to protect the species from extinction, some experts feel that captive breeding programmes may be the best strategy for future survival. Many elephants in captivity were rescued from circuses, saved from natural disasters or removed from the wild due to injury or abandonment.

Studies have clearly shown that captive animals will live longer and be more active if they are kept in an environment close to their native surroundings. The chances are, if a zoo has nothing but cement floors and metal enclosures, the animals will not do as well. Many prominent zoos now actively construct enclosures that allow animals freedom of movement, a variety of habitats and toys, and native foliage. Some zoos have even begun housing species of animals together that normally interact in the wild, such as certain types of monkeys.

Zoos are not a perfect solution for conservation; they can be endlessly improved as we better understand how to treat animals. They are undeniably helpful in repopulating dwindling animal species and encouraging a conservationist outlook, but they are unquestionably primitive in their treatment of some animals. Hopefully, animal activists and zoo proponents will continue to work together, finding ways to create the best environment for captive animals in breeding and repopulation efforts.

www.wisegeek.com/are-zoos-bad-for-animals.htm

Reading: activity 2

The words below appear in the text you have just read. What do they refer to in the text? Try to explain these using your own words.

1 wealth and power

2 conservation and education

3 confinement

4 roam, stand still

5 strain, chronic injury

6 ivory, leather and meat

7 breeding programmes, survival

8 circuses, natural disasters, injury and abandonment

9 cement floors, metal enclosures

10 a variety of habitats, toys and native foliage

11 repopulating, primitive treatment

12 animal activists and zoo proponents

Writing: activity 1

Using your ideas from the previous activity, answer the following questions.

Introductory paragraph

1 Which ideas appear in the introductory paragraph? Why?

2 What is the general opinion stated in the introductory paragraph?

3 Is there a rhetorical question in the introductory paragraph? Can you think of a question you could use in the first paragraph?

Second paragraph

4 Are the ideas in this paragraph for or against keeping animals in zoos?

5 What is the criticism in this paragraph?

Third paragraph

6 How does this paragraph start? What is the function of this linker?

7 Are the ideas in this paragraph for or against keeping animals in zoos?

8 What examples are given in support of zoos?

Fourth paragraph

9 What kinds of zoos are contrasted here? Why?

Concluding paragraph

10 Is the conclusion a one-sided opinion, or a balanced opinion? Why?

Writing: activity 2

Read the following exam-type question and identify what you have to do.

As part of the Earth Day celebration, you have been discussing the idea of keeping animals in zoos. You have now decided to write an article for the school magazine.

Study tip:
Before you start writing

Before you start writing, it is important to think for a short while. You should try and think of some ideas and plan in what order you want to write those ideas.

Also, think about how many paragraphs you need to use in your writing and the ideas you want to include in each paragraph.

This will make your writing more organised and easier to read for other people.

Here are some comments which have been mentioned in your class discussion.

Zoos wrongly teach children that keeping animals in captivity for entertainment is acceptable.

The majority of zoos provide a safe and enriched environment for animals that would otherwise become extinct in the wild.

Many animals need a lot of space to move around. They don't get this in zoos.

When children go to zoos, they learn a lot about animals and the problems these animals face in the wild.

Write an article for your school magazine giving your views.

Your article should be between 100 and 150 words long.

The comments above may give you some ideas and you should try to include ideas of your own.

Writing: activity 3

In groups, try to think of some more ideas. Look at the speech bubbles in activity 2 and try to add your own ideas. Then write them down using the headings shown below. After you have finished, compare your ideas with other groups.

Introductory paragraph:

Rhetorical question:

Ideas against:

Ideas for:

Conclusion:

Writing: activity 4

Now you are ready to write your article. Try to use some of the words you learnt in Vocabulary 3.

Writing: activity 5

Here are some more topics connected with animals. Choose one of them and write an article for homework. Follow the same plan as in activity 3.

A It is very important for children to keep an animal as a pet.

B We spend far too much money on trying to save endangered animals. Very often we can't save them and it's a waste of money.

C Everyone should become a vegetarian. It's healthy and we wouldn't have to kill any animals.

D Rich people should give some of their money to charity, or other good causes.

Summary

Can you remember …

- and name at least **four** endangered species?
- what the opposite of 'in the wild' is?
- the meaning of the following words: *to diminish*; *poaching*; *to become extinct*; *to spot*?
- **three** phrases you can use to ask for clarification?
- what information about verbs we can learn from a dictionary?
- the difference between a state verb and an action verb?
- which verb is **not** a state verb: *to love*; *to study*; *to believe*; *to know*?
- what the mistake is in the following sentence? 'I've been knowing him for three years.'

- what tense we commonly use with the following time expressions: *for four months*; *many times*; *never*; *since this morning*; *always*? Can you make a sentence with each of them?
- **two** common reasons why animals become endangered?
- the words that mean: 'to work very hard'; 'a guess about something that may happen in the future'; 'easily hurt'?
- why the following pairs of words were used in the article about zoos: 'conservation and education'; 'roam and stand still'; 'toys and native foliage'?
- what you should do before you start writing?

Progress check

Go back to the Objectives at the beginning of the chapter and assess your progress. Use the symbols below to show how confident you feel about your learning progress.

I am very good at this. ✓ ✓

I am OK, but I need a bit more practice. ✓

I can't do this yet and I need to look at this section again. ✗

Chapter 10:
Achievements

Objectives

In this chapter, you will learn and practise:

- reading skills – note-taking about a famous person
- speaking skills – discussing the topic of famous women, education and achievements
- listening skills – matching six speakers to reasons why they admire somebody
- writing skills – writing a summary about somebody's achievements and difficulties in life; writing an informal letter about an achievement, using the correct register.

You will also learn and practise the following language skills:

- narrative tenses: past simple, past continuous and past perfect
- phrasal verbs
- fixed expressions to talk about success and failure in life.

You will 'Activate your English' by:

- describing a personal event from your life
- talking about personal achievements.

Chapter 10: Achievements

📖 Reading and ✏ writing

Pre-reading activity

In small groups, look at the photos of some famous women. Do you know who they are? Where do they come from? What are their achievements? Which of the women did / has done the most for us, in your opinion?

Reading: activity 1

Scan the text about Maria Montessori and answer the questions below.

1 Who was she?

2 What does the following information mean in the text?

- 31st
- 14
- 1896
- 60
- 1925
- the 60s
- Rome
- the USA
- India
- the Netherlands

Maria Montessori

Maria Montessori was born in a provincial town, in Italy, on 31st August 1870. Her parents were well educated and quite well off. At that time, many people still had quite traditional ideas about women and their role in society. It was believed that the only three acceptable roles for women were working with children, looking after the house or living in a convent.

As a very young girl, Maria broke away from those prescribed rules and limitations. Her family moved to Rome when Maria turned 14 and, as there were no technical schools for girls at that time, she started attending a boys' school where she developed her love for maths and science, especially biology. She often had to face opposition from her father, from her teachers and male students, but she had support from her mother. Despite all the difficulties, she managed to graduate with high honours from the Medical School of the University of Rome in 1896. This was a great achievement and she went on to become the first female doctor in Italy.

As a doctor, Maria chose to specialise in paediatrics and psychiatry. While she was teaching at the Medical School of the University of Rome, she came into contact with a lot of children from poor and disadvantaged families who came to the free clinics attached to the medical school. She frequently observed that intelligence presented itself in different forms in all children in spite of their socio-economic background.

In 1900 Montessori became the director of a school for mentally ill children. Immediately, Maria and her colleagues introduced changes to how these children were treated. Maria believed that these children needed stimulation through a variety of activities which boosted their self-esteem. She dismissed anybody who showed little or no respect for her patients. Maria also battled a lack of trained staff to help her care for these children. That is why she taught most children to care for themselves and for other fellow patients. The improvement in her young patients was remarkable, and she decided to try and spread her success by giving speeches throughout Europe. She continued to work with the children and many of them, after reaching adolescence, managed to pass the standard exams taken in the public schools in Italy. Maria suggested that every newborn baby had an intellectual potential which needed to be developed, something that schools in those days were failing to do.

Maria wanted to expand her research and work with more children. Sadly, the Ministry of Education didn't approve of her work and denied her access to teaching children in public schools. However, in 1907, the Italian government gave her permission to work with young people from the slums. She was in charge of 60 children who were between the ages of one and six. This 'Children's House' was, in fact, a day care centre and Maria had to start teaching in appalling conditions. On the first day the children displayed aggressive and impatient behaviour. Maria started teaching the older children to help out with everyday activities and introduced puzzles and stimulating activities for all the children. The children were immediately interested and their behaviour changed dramatically.

Montessori's teaching method is based on close observation of a child's behaviour. Maria encouraged teachers to stand back and follow the child's natural interest. When she was criticised, she would reply: 'The children taught me how to teach them'. Her findings spread throughout Europe and the USA, and by 1925 there were more than 1000 of her schools in the USA. Unfortunately, when World War II started, her ideas faded away and Maria had to flee to India.

However, she continued to work and she put together a programme known as 'Education for Peace'. She was nominated twice for the Nobel Peace Prize for her work on this project. She died in 1952 in the Netherlands. Her schools became popular again in the 60s and her teaching methods 'follow the child' are still used nowadays all over the world.

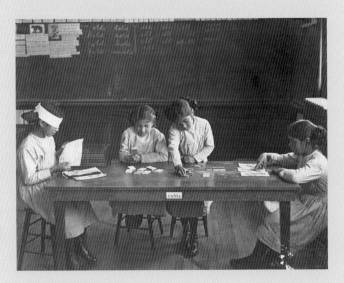

🔖 Vocabulary 1

The words below come from the article. In two groups, A and B, check the meanings in an English dictionary. Then work with somebody from the other group and swap the definitions you found in the dictionary.

Group A

- a convent (noun)
- prescribed rules (adjective)
- to boost somebody's self-esteem (phrase)
- to dismiss somebody (verb)
- to battle something (verb)
- a lack of something (noun)

Group B

- to approve of something (verb)
- to deny access to (phrase)
- slums (noun)
- appalling (adjective)
- to flee (verb)
- to fade away (phrasal verb)

Reading: activity 2

You have decided to tell your classmates about the work of Maria Montessori. For your talk you need to prepare some notes. Read the article again and make your notes under each of the headings below.

Difficulties Maria faced:

- ....
- ....

Children Maria worked with:

- ....
- ....

Maria's achievements:

- ....
- ....
- ....

Writing: activity 1

Imagine that you have given your talk about Maria Montessori and her work. It has been a great success and your teacher has asked you to write a summary for the school magazine to celebrate Teachers' Day. Look at your notes in Reading activity 2. Using the ideas in your notes, write a summary about Maria's achievements.

Your summary should be about 70 words long (and no more than 80 words long). You should use your own words as far as possible.

Writing: activity 2

Look at the sample answer by a student. The answer is good, but it has some missing words. What are they?

Maria Montessori was … [1] educator whose teaching methods are still followed around … [2] world today. She was also … [3] first woman doctor in Italy. She had to fight off … .[4] lot of opposition and criticism. Despite this, she had great success with patients and students. Moreover, her teachings became popular and 1000 of her schools opened in … . [5] USA. Last, but not least, she received two Nobel Peace Prize nominations.

(70 words)

Writing: activity 3

Read the complete summary again and underline the linkers that the student uses. What function do they have in the summary?

Writing: activity 4

Look at your notes in Reading activity 2 again. Using the ideas, write a summary about the difficulties Maria had to face. In your summary, try to use the linkers from the previous activity.

Your summary should be about 70 words long (and no more than 80 words long). You should use your own words as far as possible.

Writing: activity 5

When you have finished, swap your summaries with your partner. Check their summary against the list of points below.

- Do they talk about difficulties?
- Do they use appropriate linkers?
- Do they use their own words?
- Are their ideas in a logical order?
- Is the summary the correct length?
- Do they use correct grammar, including correct articles?
- Do they spell words correctly?

Speaking

Work in two groups. Each group should work on one of the groups outlined below and discuss the points. Then report back for a class discussion. Don't forget to provide reasons for your opinions.

Group A: Famous women

- What famous woman do you admire? Why?
- Do any famous women come from your country?
- What are they famous for?
- In what areas are women mostly famous? Give examples.
- Do you think there should be more women in other areas? Why? Why not?
- Should there be more male *or* female teachers? Why? Why not?

Group B: Education

- What do you like about being a student?
- Do you think it's easier to be a student nowadays? Give examples.
- Would you like to be a student in Maria Montessori's time? Why? Why not?
- What classroom activities do you enjoy? Why?
- Do you think there is too much emphasis on academic success and not enough focus on practical skills and hands-on experience?
- Do you feel that schools prepare young people well enough for life after school?

Language focus

Narrative tenses

Analysis

Read the following text. Then close the book and tell your partner what the text is about.

Key term: narrative tenses

We use narrative tenses when we talk about past events. We use them, for example, when we tell a story. The most common tenses are: past simple, past continuous and past perfect.

For example, *When we* **got** (past simple) *to the cinema, the film* **had already started** (past perfect). *It was dark and as I* **was trying** (past continuous) *to get to my seat, I tripped over something.*

My parents decided to move to Dubai for work when I was 11 years old. At first I was excited, but then the reality hit me. I had to say goodbye to my school, to my friends and my grandparents, all the people who I love very much. On my first day at my new school, I just wanted to run away. Everyone tried to speak to me, but in a language I didn't understand. Luckily, I got to know Yusuf who was from Egypt. When I first saw him, he sat quietly at his desk and read something. I was sitting next to him and asking him in English what his name was. We got on like a house on fire and became really good friends. He already studied at the school for three years when I started. He also knew Arabic so could translate for me. Before meeting him, I only learnt the words 'Hello' and 'Thank you', but Yusuf taught me more. I also started attending Arabic classes for beginners and was soon able to have conversations with other students. Now I'm fluent and life seems to be good. I still miss my old friends though, and my grandparents, of course.

Read the text again. There are four mistakes in tenses. Can you underline them?

What should the correct tense be? Write out the correct sentences.

Now work in pairs and answer the following questions.

1   Which tense do we use to describe a scene?

2   Which tense do we use to say what happened?

3   Which tense do we use to say that something started/happened earlier than something else?

Look at the following sentences and answer the questions.

4   When I got to school, the lesson had started.

    Was I late?

5   When I got to school, the lesson started.

    Was I late?

6 When I came in, Johan was singing his favourite song.

What started first?

Did I hear the beginning?

7 When I came in, Johan sang his favourite song.

What happened first?

Did I hear the beginning?

8 When I got home, my sister had cleaned the whole flat.

Did I see her clean the flat?

Was she still cleaning when I got home?

Practice

Exercise 1
Complete the sentences with the correct tense. Use the verbs in the brackets.

1 As Monika .... (leave) school yesterday, it .... (start) to rain.

2 As soon as I .... (get) off the bus, I .... (realise) that I .... (leave) my umbrella on the bus.

3 When I .... (see) her in the street, I .... (know) I .... (meet) her somewhere before.

4 When I .... (enter) the room, everybody .... (laugh) at Federico's joke.

5 Before the exam date, my brother .... (do) a lot of revision non-stop.

6 When I .... (fly) to see my aunt in Kuala Lumpur, I .... (feel) very scared. I .... (never fly) on my own before.

7 On the day of the exam I .... (oversleep) because I .... (not set) the alarm clock.

8 When they .... (be) little, they .... (never like) to listen to classical music.

9 The sun .... (shine) and everybody .... (enjoy) themselves by the pool when we .... (arrive) there.

10 After Tatyana .... (tell) me, I .... (can't) stop thinking about it.

Exercise 2
Work in pairs and complete the sentences with your own ideas.

1 As I was leaving the flat, …

2 When I got home, …

3 While I was doing my homework, …

4 First I went shopping and then …

138

5   After I'd been studying for several hours, …

6   It wasn't until then that I realised that …

7   I was very happy because …

8   I'd been living there for many years when I realised that …

9   As I sat down to watch the TV, …

10 I didn't want to leave the party because …

Exercise 3
Look at some of the words taken from the paragraph in the Analysis section. Can you put them in the correct order without looking at the original text? Work in groups and retell the story using the words and the correct tenses. When you are happy with all the details, write the story.

Then read the other stories done by other groups. Which story was closest to the original story? What details did your classmates forget to include?

Yusuf	Arabic	Dubai	fluent	run away
a house on fire	excited	miss	three years	quietly
Egypt	beginners	his name	11 years old	'Hello' and 'Thank you'

Activate your English
Work in groups of three. Choose one of the topics and spend a few moments thinking about what you want to say. Then tell the other two students about what happened, but don't say which topic you have chosen. Your partners have to listen very carefully and say which topic you were talking about.

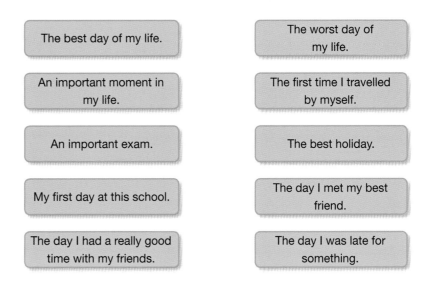

The best day of my life.

The worst day of my life.

An important moment in my life.

The first time I travelled by myself.

An important exam.

The best holiday.

My first day at this school.

The day I met my best friend.

The day I had a really good time with my friends.

The day I was late for something.

🔊 Listening

Pre-listening activity

In pairs, look at the pictures together and discuss the following questions.

- What kind of things did the people achieve?
- How do you think they feel?
- What difficulties do you think they had to overcome?
- What qualities do you need to achieve these goals?
- Would you like to achieve the same?

Listening: activity 1

Listen to six speakers in track 20 and say what achievements they talk about.

Which one do you think is the greatest achievement? Why?

Listening: activity 2

Listen to the six speakers again. Why does each of them admire the person they're talking about? For each speaker 1–6, choose from the list A–G. Which reason does each speaker express? Use each letter only once. There is one extra letter which you do not need to use.

Speaker 1:	**A**	Consideration for others
Speaker 2:	**B**	Confidence
Speaker 3:	**C**	Perseverance
Speaker 4:	**D**	Imagination
Speaker 5:	**E**	Patience
Speaker 6:	**F**	Bravery
	G	Wisdom

Listening: activity 3
Listen again and write down at least one phrase that helped you decide on the correct answer in activity 2.

See Transcript 19 at the back of the book.

 # Vocabulary 2

Phrasal verbs and other fixed expressions

Exercise 1
Look at Transcript 19 at the back of the book and find the words that mean the same as the following:

Speaker 1:
• to stop doing something because you don't want to do it any more (phrasal verb)
• to begin again from the very start (fixed expression)
• when ambitions become reality (fixed expression)

Speaker 2:
• to stay calm and not panic (fixed expression)

Speaker 3:
• to start an activity (phrasal verb)

Speaker 4:
• to admire and respect somebody (phrasal verb)
• to cope with a difficult situation and to survive it (phrasal verb)

Speaker 5:
• to think of something / invent something (phrasal verb)
• to become an adult (phrasal verb)

Exercise 2
Look at some more collocations and idioms we use when we talk about success or failure in life. In pairs match the correct halves. Which phrases are used to talk about success and which ones about failure?

Look up unfamiliar words or phrases in an English dictionary.

1	It was nothing	A	miserably
2	It was a resounding	B	excellent progress
3	to pass my exam	C	downfall
4	It was a total	D	success
5	to enjoy the fruits of	E	a storm
6	to fail	F	to write home about
7	My dreams came	G	disaster
8	to make	H	with flying colours
9	It went down	I	crashing down
10	it led to his	J	your hard work

Exercise 3

What are the missing words? In pairs complete the sentences. Then, using the questions in the exercise, make conversations with your classmates.

1   Who do you ……………….. up to in your family? Why?

2   Have you ever …………… up something because you couldn't continue? What and why?

3   Do you find it easy to ……………. up with solutions to problems? When was the last time you had to do that?

4   Can you think of an event at your school that …………… down a storm? Give details.

5   Have you ever ………………... something miserably? What do you think was the reason?

6   Would you ever ……………… up a voluntary job? What sort of voluntary work would you like to do? Do you think enough people do voluntary work? Give examples.

7   In your opinion why do people's dreams ……………….. crashing down? Give examples.

8   What would you advise students to do in order to …………….. their IGCSE exams with ………………... colours?

9   Do you think you can …………….. your cool in stressful situations? Have you ever been in a stressful situation before? What happened?

10 Can you think of anything you've done that was a resounding …………………..? What was it and what happened? Give details.

Activate your English

In small groups, choose one of the topics to talk about your achievements. Spend two to three minutes planning what you want to say, but don't make any written notes. Then tell your group about your achievements.

In your talk mention the following.

- What it was.
- When it happened.
- What you had to do to achieve it.
- Who/what helped you.
- Was it an easy/difficult task?
- What the result was.
- How it made you feel.

Project

You are going to give a presentation to the class about a person you admire. Prepare notes for your presentation and then deliver it to the class. Notes for your presentation should cover the following points.

Study tip:
Giving a presentation
Remember that it is always more exciting for the audience when you include pictures or interesting facts. Also, make sure you look at the audience when delivering your presentation and don't read out the information from a piece of paper – say it in your own words.

You could use cue cards to help you remember what you want to talk about.

1   Introduction.
    - Name
    - Who they are
    - Where from
    - When born/lived
    - Interesting facts about their life
2   Their achievement(s) and how they succeeded.
3   Why you admire them.

When you have finished your presentation, don't forget to ask the audience if they have any questions.

After you've heard a few presentations, have a discussion about the people mentioned by your classmates. Work in groups and discuss the following.

- Who was the bravest?
- Who had the most difficult life?
- Who changed our lives for the better and why?
- Who encountered the most problems?
- Who you would most like to meet and why?

 # Writing

Writing: activity 1

Read the exam-type question and say what you have to include in your letter.

You have recently achieved something special in your life and you want to share your experience with a friend.

Write a letter to a friend about the achievement.

In your letter you should:

- say what your achievement was and why it is important to you
- explain how you prepared for it
- describe the most difficult moment.

The pictures in the pre-listening activity may give you some ideas, and you should try to use some ideas of your own. **Your letter should be between 100 to 150 words long**. Do not write an address.

Writing: activity 2

Read the two sample letters. Did the students answer all the bullet points in the question? What information did they include for each point? Underline the details in the text.

Sample A:

Dear Benoit,

Thanks for your last letter. It was really great to hear from you and to read about your success in the exam. You must be so relieved that it's all over.

Speaking of which, I'm dying to tell you about my great success. I think I told you a while back that I'd been training for the big tennis tournament at our school. You'll never believe this, but I won. It's very important to me because I always thought I wasn't good enough to win anything. Thanks to this achievement, my self-confidence got a big boost. I'd been training really hard for several months before the tournament. I also made sure that I only ate healthy food to get more energy. To build up my stamina, I went jogging every morning. This may surprise you, but the most difficult part wasn't the actual match, but the weather. On the day when I arrived, the sun was so bright and the temperature had reached the high twenties. It was an outdoor tournament and, as you can imagine, it was boiling hot.

To celebrate I've invited all my friends to go out for a meal. Fancy coming too? It'd be great.

Hope you can come.

All the best,

Karin

Sample B:

Hi Jenya,

I passed a very difficult test yesterday. I studied hard for it. I went to the library every day before the exam. I'm very happy now because the good test result will help me to get to a good university. The whole test was difficult. The time limit was very short and I had to hurry. I made some mistakes. The result was good. I'm pleased.

Love,

Irina

145

Study tip:
Make your writing more interesting

To make your writing more interesting, think about using the following.

- Different linkers to link your ideas together and make your sentences more complex and natural-sounding.
- A range of tenses (e.g. narrative tenses).
- A range of adjectives and verbs.
- Interesting expressions (e.g. collocations, fixed expressions, etc.).
- Examples to support what you say.

Study tip:
Using the right register

In English we use different registers. **Formal register** is the one that is commonly used when we speak to someone we don't know or to someone we respect. **Informal register** is used when you talk to your friends and family.

It is important that you use the correct register otherwise you might offend somebody you don't know, or you might sound arrogant to your friends.

For example, if you say: '**Can you give me a hand?**' to somebody you don't know, they might think you're a bit impolite. In this situation it might be better to say something like: '**Excuse me, I was wondering if you could help me.**'

This also applies when you write. You have to think about who will read your letter and then choose the most suitable register.

Writing: activity 3

Work in pairs and compare the two sample letters. Which candidate did the following?

1 Wrote in the correct style. (a letter)
2 Used an informal register.
3 Used paragraphs.
4 Used linkers.
5 Used complex sentences.
6 Used the correct grammar.
7 Used a range of grammatical structures.
8 Used a range of vocabulary.
9 Spelt words correctly.
10 Used the correct punctuation.

Writing: activity 4

Discuss the following questions in pairs.

1 Which sample letter is more interesting to read? Why?
2 Look at the two highlighted phrases and one grammatical structure in Sample A. Why did the student use them?
3 Can you use this type of vocabulary when you're writing to somebody you don't know? Why? Why not?

Using the sample letter you found more interesting to read, make a list of some more interesting phrases or grammatical structures.

 Vocabulary 3

Informal expressions

Scan Sample A and find the words that mean the same as the following words or phrases:

1 happy after a stressful situation has finished
2 it's finished
3 I really want to
4 some time ago
5 helped me to feel better about myself
6 to improve something bit by bit
7 extremely hot
8 would you like to …?

Writing: activity 5

Look at Sample B again. In small groups, rewrite the letter making the sentences more complex, adding some more linkers, and using a range of tenses and interesting vocabulary. Then compare your answers with other groups. Whose answer is the best?

Writing: activity 6

Now write your own answer to the question in activity 1. Make sure that you include complex sentences with interesting linkers and vocabulary and a range of tenses. When you have finished, work with a partner and discuss each other's answers.

Summary

Can you remember ...

- at least **three** of Maria Montessori's achievements?
- the meaning of the following: 'to battle something'; 'slums'; 'to flee'?
- **one** linker we use to add extra information and **one** linker to express contrasting ideas? Can you make a sentence with each linker?
- what narrative tenses are?
- what is wrong with this sentence? 'When we had dinner, our neighbour had rung the doorbell.'
- how to use narrative tenses? Talk about what you did yesterday using narrative tenses.

- what these three phrasal verbs mean: 'to give up'; 'to get through'; 'to look up to'?
- what the missing words are in these expressions? 'It was nothing to ………….. home about'; 'It went …………. a storm'; 'I've passed my exams with flying ……………'
- **one** more expression for success and **one** for failure?
- how to make your writing more interesting?
- which informal expressions mean: 'to improve'; 'some time ago'; 'I really want to ...'? Can you make sentences with all three?

Progress check

Go back to the Objectives at the beginning of this chapter and assess your progress. Use the symbols below to show how confident you feel about your learning progress.

I am very good at this.	✓ ✓
I am OK, but I need a bit more practice.	✓
I can't do this yet and I need to look at this section again.	✗

Appendix

Audio scripts

Transcript 1 (track 2)

Recording 1

Teacher: OK, Mehdi. It is often said that good manners are disappearing these days, especially amongst young people. Can you remember the last time you helped somebody?

Mehdi: Yes.

Teacher: When was it and what happened?

Mehdi: It was this morning. I gave up my seat on the bus for an elderly person.

Teacher: That's very good of you. How did it make you feel?

Mehdi: Good. I always do it.

Teacher: Do you think people often give up their seat?

Mehdi: No, not very often.

Teacher: OK, let us look at the second prompt …

Recording 2

Examiner: OK, Eleni. It is often said that good manners are disappearing these days, especially amongst young people. Can you remember the last time you helped somebody?

Eleni: Yes, I can. It was yesterday. I was on my way home. I take the train and there was this lady with a baby. She was trying to get off the train with a buggy, but there's quite a gap between the train and the platform and she struggled to get the buggy out. I asked her if she needed a hand and helped her with the buggy.

Examiner: Good for you, Eleni. How did it make you feel?

Eleni: It made me feel very happy. I like helping others. I always like to help others because one day I might need their help.

Examiner: Could you explain that a bit more, Eleni.

Eleni: Certainly. What I mean is – we shouldn't just expect help from others. We should make sure that we also give help to other people. I think it's nice when we're civil to each other.

Examiner: That's a very good idea, Eleni. Now let us look at the second prompt …

Transcript 2 (track 3)

Recording 1

When I first came to the UK, I thought I'd miss my bike because at home I go biking almost every day. But actually, it's the sunshine I wish I could have more of. I'm also sad I can't buy German bread. I can't get used to the sliced bread here. But what I really enjoy is fish and chips. I know it's not the most healthy food, but it tastes so good. I just love it. My friend, on the other hand, loves cottage pie.

Recording 2

After my first lesson in this language school, I was nervous. I didn't know anybody and everybody looked so serious. But after a few days, I realised the teachers were really friendly and helpful, which made me more relaxed. In the afternoon, when we finish our lessons, students can meet and study in the library. But I personally prefer revising in the café, which is round the corner from the school. I do my homework there because I can use their wi-fi.

Recording 3

Once I went to my friend's house and his mum offered me some tea. It was a very cold day and I thought, 'Oh, this will be nice'. What I didn't know was that in England most people drink their tea with milk. When I got the drink, I thought to myself, 'Maybe she misunderstood me and gave me a mug of milk,' and I drank it. I'm sorry to say that I really didn't enjoy it. Back home we always put lemon and honey in our tea, which is much nicer than using sugar.

Recording 4

I'm really close to my family. Now I'm studying abroad so I miss them a lot, especially my brother. We're like twins and being away from him is really the hardest thing. We keep in touch via Skype. I also phone my sister, but not that often as she sometimes visits me so we can catch up face to face. My family lives in a different time zone to me. I'd love to use Skype right after the lessons, or in the evening, but for practical reasons it has to be in the morning. Sometimes it has to be very quick because I need to rush off to school.

Transcript 3 (track 4)

1   It <u>has been</u> repaired.

2   It <u>was</u> made very popular in the sixties.

3   They <u>were</u> carved out of radishes.

4   It <u>can</u> be used as a decoration.

5   Yes, it <u>has.</u>

6   Yes, it <u>was.</u>

7   Yes, they <u>were.</u>

8   Yes, it <u>can.</u>

Transcript 4 (track 5)

Interviewer: This week we've been talking about festivals around the world and the people who help to make them happen. In the studio with me today is Dana Ferreira, a famous samba choreographer, and she'll be talking to us about her background and also her favourite festival in Brazil – the Carnival, of course. Hello Dana.

Dana: Thanks for having me. Well, let me start by telling you a bit about me. My parents are originally from Brazil and that's where I was born. But then they had to move for their jobs to Portugal and that's where I grew up and still live. I left Portugal for a few years to study in Paris, but after graduation and one job I returned.

My father wasn't very happy about my career choice. He always thought I'd follow in his footsteps and study law. I considered this for a while, but then went with my heart and chose to study dance and choreography. After completing my university studies, I was offered a place at the Théâtre du Monde, but this wasn't my first job. I had to earn a living to support myself at university, so I helped with a variety of dance productions in schools. It was a very interesting job and I got invaluable first-hand experience working as a choreographer. I preferred that to active dancing. I always looked to the Brazilian carnivals for inspiration, but never went there myself until recently. Being Brazilian myself, I was always fascinated by the Carnival. I tried to go on more occasions, for example in 2010, but there was always a job that needed finishing first. And then when it did happen in 2014, it was just out of this world. Everyone should go and have this great experience. The explosion of colours and sounds is just unbelievable.

Now I'd like to focus on the Carnival itself. It's held annually, approximately 40 days before Easter and it goes on for about five days, but many Brazilians carry on for up to 10 days sometimes. Although carnivals are held in cities all around Brazil, the Carnival in Rio is believed to be the biggest and richest of them all. This doesn't mean, however, that the rest of the carnivals are boring, quite the opposite.

During the Carnival in Rio, the people's parade consists of different samba schools, who select as many as 5000 participants, and they all compete for the title of the 'Carnival Champion'. It's taken very seriously and they prepare for it several months in advance.

First of all, each school settles on a theme. This could be from nature, music, sport or art, but they all have to be Brazilian themes. Then they create their own costumes, songs and choreography. And they just rehearse over and over again until it's all perfect.

But what actually happens on the day? The judges have to decide on the winner and I wouldn't like to be them. It's a very hard job. All the participants are just so wonderful. However, the judges focus on the following criteria: the costumes, rhythm, timing and the response from the audience. They also award the participants with points between zero and ten.

When I came back home from my Brazilian trip, I was so fascinated I wanted to find out more about the origins. The roots lie in ancient traditions from Africa and Portugal. Apparently, in 1723 the immigrants from islands like Madeira brought the carnival over to Brazil. Around the year 1930 it reached a peak of popularity when samba schools started to appear in Rio. Thanks to the local people, it gradually mixed with more local elements until it finally became the Carnival we all know and love today.

Interviewer: Well, thank you very much for this …

Transcript 5 (track 6)

Speaker 1:
When I was little, I went to the cinema with my father to watch the film *Gorillas in the Mist* based on the life of Dian Fossey. She fought very hard to protect the mountain gorillas against hunters and save them from extinction. I was so emotional after the film and couldn't stop thinking about it. Since that moment I've always wanted to be involved in a project to continue what Dian Fossey started. And guess what! I'm getting ready to join an expedition that is going to Africa next year. So, I need to start preparing now really. I'm so excited. Plus, I've never been to Africa before.

Speaker 2:
My friend Ivan told me about this championship that happens in Siberia in one of the lakes. Basically, what they do, is they swim in icy cold water. I thought it was really unusual and wanted to try it. I also heard that swimming in icy water is supposed to boost your immune system and improve your blood circulation. I was looking forward to it and thought I'd be very healthy afterwards. Sadly, one week after I came back, I got the worst flu ever. I guess the good benefits of icy water didn't work on me so I'm not sure if I want to repeat the experience.

Speaker 3:
I felt very lonely when I started my new school so my friend Elke suggested a whale-watching trip near New Zealand to meet new people. I thought – why not? We didn't just watch whales swimming around the ship. We even took photos of the whales and then looked at them to see if any of the whales were injured. It really made me forget my troubles. I went there in March, which is a good month for watching orcas, the killer whales. Now I'm home and already planning another journey for October which is the end of the season for watching other types of whales.

Speaker 4:
I've always been fascinated by the Himalayas. When I was younger, I joined a mountaineering group and went to the Alps and the Pyrenees to train to climb mountains. It taught me never to go unprepared. It wasn't until last year though that I managed to go to the Himalayas. We decided to climb the tenth highest mountain in the world – Annapurna in Nepal. During the climb it got a bit lonely at times. You can't really talk to anybody and in the evening you are so tired you just fall asleep. But it was well worth it.

Speaker 5:
In my life I've done a lot of scuba-diving with our local club. My father wanted to surprise me for my eighteenth birthday, so he bought me a trip to the Great Barrier Reef and a scuba-diving course with professional divers. The reef has so many types of fish you never knew existed. Unfortunately, the reef is being polluted by carbon dioxide and the water is becoming too acidic. When my time at the reef ended, I decided to apply for a job over there. I'm also planning to settle down there and possibly study marine biology. I hope it all works out.

Speaker 6:
I love extreme sports. That's why I decided to cross Death Valley in California in my car. I didn't want to do it on my own as you can feel quite isolated and lonely, and you never know when you might need help. That's the reason why I asked my best friend to come with me. Luckily, we managed to cross Death Valley without any big problems, but I must say what I never realised was how cold it gets at night – sometimes even below zero. I was really freezing because I didn't bring any warm clothes. You'd never believe that a desert can get that cold, would you? But now I can say I've done it and can start thinking about the next new challenge.

Transcript 6 (track 7)

1 white*board*
2 wheel*chair*
3 drinking *water*
4 rain*fall*
5 space *shuttle*
6 Face*book*
7 basket*ball*
8 bank*note*
9 chop*sticks*
10 dead*line*
11 gold*fish*
12 key*board*
13 pick*pocket*
14 sky*scraper*
15 sun*shine*

Transcript 7 (track 8)

Recording 1

self-service
postgraduate
non-judgemental
oversleep
overeat
postproduction
self-discipline
antisocial
underpaid
self-confident
non-smoking

Recording 2

oversleep / overeat / underpaid
self-service / non-smoking
postgraduate / self-discipline / self-confident
non-judgemental / postproduction / anti-social

Transcript 8 (track 9)

Interviewer: Good morning everybody and welcome to our weekly programme about people in science. Everybody in the studio is very excited because we have a very special guest with us today – an astronaut in training, Tim Mason. Hi Tim!

Can you tell us something about yourself and what you have to do to become an astronaut?

Tim: Hi. As you said, my name is Tim Mason and I'm an astronaut. My parents come from Canada and that's where my brother was born. When he was 6 years old, they all moved to the United States, where I was born two years later. When I was 10, I became interested in space and wanted to become an astronaut. When I turned 18, my dream was to train at the Johnson Space Center. My parents, however, didn't think it was a realistic ambition and wanted me to work in the family's restaurant as a waiter. I considered it for a while, but then went to university to become a teacher. I was a teacher for three years, but it wasn't the right career path for me so I finally decided to pursue my real ambition to become an astronaut.

I started my training at the Johnson Space Center in Houston. I think you should know that the centre goes back to 1961 when it was formally established, but wasn't open for business at that time. This happened two years later in 1963. In 1973 it was named after a former president, Lyndon Baines Johnson, who was also from Texas. The centre has had a leading role in projects such as Apollo, Gemini and the International Space Station programmes. Around 370 astronauts have been trained there. Fifty of these astronauts were from other countries.

There are many stages of training you have to go through before you can call yourself an astronaut. The training is really tough, physically and mentally. After the initial training and selection process, you go through stage one. The candidates that are selected come from all corners of society from teachers, scientists, the military or engineers.

The first stage is the basic training, but don't be fooled by the name – it's not basic at all. It lasts for two years and you have to read a lot of different manuals about space shuttles and space station systems, and go through simulations and survival training on land and in water.

One of the biggest obstacles astronauts in general have to overcome is weightlessness, but the real challenge for me was getting used to the restricted diet. All candidates are obliged to obtain a scuba-diving certificate and do a swimming test as the closest you can get to the state of weightlessness is when you are underwater. You really need a good physique because all candidates are required to swim three lengths of a 25-metre pool non-stop and then swim the same distance again, but with a flight suit and shoes on. You can take as long as you want, but you mustn't stop. That is tough. This is really embarrassing, but when I was getting ready to do this test, I was so nervous I forgot to put the shoes on and swam in just my socks. Unfortunately, I had to do the test again.

Astronauts are taught how to do tasks in zero gravity; this could be an everyday activity such as eating, or a more complicated activity, for example, repairing control panels or walking in space. All this training happens in huge water tanks at the centre.

After this training you are an official astronaut, but the training doesn't end there. You enter the second stage. Now you are assigned a mentor, an experienced astronaut, who passes on their knowledge and experience. I was very lucky with my mentor. We got on really well. He was really patient even though I often got things wrong and it would be understandable if he got angry. What I appreciated above all, though, was his friendly attitude. That really helped me a lot because as a trainee, you must know how to deal with a lot of things – for example, all the activities during pre-launch, the launch itself and then being in orbit, coming back to Earth and landing.

Then you enter an advanced stage in your training which normally takes around ten months. By now you will have chosen what assignment in space you intend to focus on and the role you want to undertake. All your remaining training is specific to your space mission. You **can** choose what area of work you want to dedicate yourself to.

I have now entered my final stage of the advanced programme. I originally planned to be an engineer, but given my background I opted for the role of research scientist.

Interviewer: Well, all the best from all of us, Tim, and thanks again for coming today.

Transcript 9 (track 10)

Interviewer: Hello and welcome to our programme. Today we're going to be talking to Jonathon Su Park, who specialises in the areas of social networking sites and how these affect our lives. Jonathon, what do the experts say?

Jonathon: According to the latest research, social networking is one of the most popular pastimes for young people in their late teens. As this is a relatively new pastime, experts are worried about the long-term impact this may have on this generation. Also, many parents worry whether their children are safe when using the Internet and, especially, social networking sites.

Interviewer: We are all very interested in the issue of young people using the Internet and how it changes their relationships, particularly with their grandparents.

Jonathon: Yes, this is quite interesting. In the past, before the Internet was widely available, children and young people used to spend a fair amount of time with their grandparents, who helped with the children's up-bringing from time to time. They were there to answer a lot of the questions their grandchildren had. They passed on the wisdom of their generation. They would also teach them important everyday things, such as how to mend stuff or how to cook.

Interviewer: What about now? Has it changed a lot?

Jonathon: Yes, we are seeing shocking statistics in some countries that suggest that grandchildren are turning to computers for help rather than to their grandparents. Grandparents say that only one in four have been asked for help. A lot of teenagers nowadays have their own smartphone or tablet bought by their parents, so it is very easy for them to get instant answers from sites like Google. Teenagers know that their grandparents could answer their questions, but the Internet is quicker and that's what teenagers prefer.

Interviewer: So, how do the grandparents feel about this?

Jonathon: Some grandparents who took part in the research felt as if they were being replaced by these sites and the Internet in general. Their grandchildren still come and visit, but they spend the time on their electronic devices instead of interacting with them and asking about what life was like when their grandparents were young. Both groups said they loved each other just as much as before, but they are losing an important connection and this is resulting in a wider generation gap, which is really sad to see.

Interviewer: I must say it is a bit heartbreaking. Do you think this situation can still be changed?

Jonathon: Electronic devices have simply become part of our children's lives. This is something we just have to accept. A good way of trying to close this new generation gap is by encouraging grandparents to become more computer savvy. That way they can become more involved in their grandchildren's free time and offer guidance. We can't expect grandparents to rush out and buy the latest smartphone or stream films and music on their computer immediately, but we're hoping that showing more interest in modern devices will be the first step in improving relationships.

Interviewer: How does time spent on the computer fit in with our hectic modern lifestyle?

Jonathon: These days it is not just the grown-ups who have more work than they used to. It is also the teenagers. They spend much more time at school or doing homework. The demands of school are much greater so it is not surprising that teenagers don't have as much time to go out and form new friendships. The research has shown that social sites play an invaluable role in filling this gap. These days, teenagers stay in touch with their friends, make new friends, play games and even do their homework through these sites. They broaden their horizons by joining discussion blogs and sharing new music, and learn to express their empathy towards others.

Interviewer: I've never thought about social networking in this way. What about the dangers though? What can parents do to protect their children?

Jonathon: Parents should get involved in their children's online activities. Parents around the world have different opinions about how much involvement there should be. Surprisingly, only a small minority of parents think they should have full control of their children's online activities. In some countries they feel their children should be allowed to make their own decisions. However, the vast majority said that they know best when their children are ready to join social networking sites. Once their child has an account, parents should make sure that their children use privacy settings and don't share personal details like their address or contact details. Regarding passwords, children should be allowed to choose words that mean something to them. It is advisable, though, that this information is shared with the parents. There also needs to be some control over who can view their pages and who their online friends are.

Interviewer: And what does the latest research tell us about our children's needs?

Jonathon: It shows that children are very independent these days when it concerns researching information online for their school work, but parents should discuss openly what sources their children are using and how reliable the websites are. Parents should also watch out for any changes in their child's behaviour. Interestingly though, the study mainly revealed that it is still important for the children to know that they can turn to their parents and grandparents when they experience problems.

Interviewer: Well, Jonathon, I could talk to you for much longer, but sadly, we've run out of time. I'd like to thank you again and wish you …

Transcript 10 (track 11)

1 I haven't really thought about that.

2 Let me see.

3 Oh, that's a tricky question.

4 How can I put this?

Transcript 11 (track 12)

When we think about face painting today, we usually think about the colourful images that are drawn onto a child's face at places like the fair or the circus. However, that wasn't always what face painting was all about. Face painting dates back thousands of years across many different cultures and has been used for a wide variety of purposes that weren't just all for fun, such as hunting and in military battles. It's a really interesting history that most of us aren't aware of even though we all know what face painting is.

People have used face paint as a means of camouflaging themselves since ancient times. They would paint their faces using natural substances so that their skin would blend in with the natural environment around them. This was good for hunting because it meant that the animals would be less likely to notice the hunters. Hunters today may still use face paint for this same reason. Likewise, people fighting battles have used face paint to hide themselves so they could sneak up on their enemies and get really close, which would give them the element of surprise. Before a battle, warriors from certain tribes also painted symbols on their faces to show the enemy how brave they were, how many battles they had won and above all to generate fear.

Historically, there were times when face painting was used for various religious ceremonies. One strong example of this comes from a look at the history of Native American tribes in the United States. Many tribes believed that face painting with specific colours had special meanings and could be used as a spiritual tool. For example, it was believed by some that wearing green face paint would give the wearer special powers that would enable him to see well during the night.

In the past, face painting also became common in the world of live entertainment. Many different groups of people got involved with elaborate face painting to enhance costumes that were used in some types of entertainment, such as the opera, for the enjoyment of the audience.

Face painting has long been a part of the history of sports. You may want to think about the sport of American football and the face paint that is associated with that game. Alternatively, you may want to think about how face paint has been used in wrestling to help to create the appropriate character of the people who participate in that sport. Today, it is not only the participants in sports that engage in face painting. For example, at football and baseball matches, you can see fans with the colours of their team or country painted on their faces.

In the 1960s it became very popular for many adults to paint their faces with symbols of peace when attending music festivals. However, it wasn't until about 1980 that the use of face painting as a way for kids to enjoy themselves became widespread. During this time, face painting became a child's thing, the thing that we think of it as being today. It is something that is typically seen at fairs and amusement parks and markets and festivals. This is most common today in Europe and North America, although it can also be found in other countries throughout the world.

http://kathrynvercillo.hubpages.com/hub/A-Brief-History-of-Face-Painting

Transcript 12 (track 13)

Recording 1

We would like to inform all visitors that they can finally visit the east wing of our museum again from next week. This is after the renovation, which took two weeks longer than expected. The new exhibition is dedicated to the art of the Incas and you can admire not only beautiful jewellery designs and pottery, but also weapons and masks. It will be on until June and will be accompanied by talks every Thursday. We would like to remind you that the exhibition will not be open to the public on Mondays. This day is reserved for school visits only.

Recording 2

Woman: I love this café. It is very convenient. You can have a look round the exhibition and have some refreshments at the end.

Man: Yes, it's great. To be honest I didn't know about the café until last month when my neighbour mentioned it to me. My girlfriend didn't know about it either.

Woman: Really? I've been coming here for at least two years now. They have great cakes and very good coffee. But I must say I was disappointed with the sandwiches. They are not always fresh.

Man: Oh, that's good to know. So what would you like today?

Woman: I might have a slice of banana cake.

Man: Are you sure? Last time you had banana cake, you didn't like it.

Woman: OK, you're right. I'll go for the chocolate cake instead.

Recording 3

Man: Excuse me, do you work here?

Woman: Yes, how can I help you?

Man: I'm looking for the photography exhibition. Do you know where it is? I've been trying to find it for the last half an hour, but your gallery is so huge. I think I'm lost.

Woman: OK, but you'll have to tell me which photography exhibition you want to see. We have two on at the moment. One is modern photography and the other one is the National Geographic exhibition.

Man: I didn't realise there were two. Modern photography sounds good, but I'm here to see the National Geographic one.

Woman: In that case, it's on the first floor. But it's not free like the other exhibition. It costs $7.60 but today there's a special offer on so you'll only have to pay $5.50.

Man: Thank you very much for your help.

Recording 4

Hi Carmen! Pity you're not answering. I'm just calling to let you know that tomorrow I can meet you outside the museum at 2.30 p.m. Normally, the museum closes at 8 p.m., but it'll be at 6.30 tomorrow so that should give us enough time to see the exhibition. I really wanted to see the collection of famous Hollywood dresses but apparently the last day to see that is today. Shame really. I guess it's just the French posters then. They're supposed to be really beautiful. OK, that's it. Cheerio. Oh, by the way, it's Sandra.

Transcript 13 (track 14)

Speaker 1:
My favourite sport is a team sport. I like the contact with other people. You have a lot of fun hitting the ball over the net. It's a good workout too, because you have to try and keep the ball off the ground and that requires a lot of running across your half of the court.

Speaker 2:
My friend invited me to this game. I wasn't sure if I should go because I'm not really into this sport. I thought I'd just sit there and watch. But I must say it got really exciting. It was a doubles game. I'd never seen someone hit the shuttlecock so hard. One of the players got a bit angry at the umpire so there was plenty of drama too. You should come with me next time.

Speaker 3:
I'm telling you – kicking a ball on the pitch is easy compared to this. This is a really dangerous sport. When you fall, the landing is much harder. Plus, if you get hit by the puck that must really hurt. That's why everybody wears a helmet and the goalkeeper wears a special protective shield over his face. I've tried playing it and it's really difficult to follow the puck with your stick.

Transcript 14 (track 15)

Sonia: Hello, Vikram. Thank you very much for agreeing to talk to me.

Vikram: It's my pleasure, Sonia.

Sonia: Today's programme is dedicated to the Paralympics and I've always wondered how it all started.

Vikram: These days it's a global event, but that wasn't always the case. They weren't always called the Paralympics. In the early days they were called the Stoke Mandeville Games. That was when they started back in 1948. It was the same year as the first Summer Olympics in London.

Sonia: And what did these early Games involve?

Vikram: It's simple. The first Games were held for the patients at the Stoke Mandeville hospital in Aylesbury, England and the first participants were the patients who had suffered spinal injuries. Nowadays we have a lot of sports at the Paralympics – from swimming to cycling. During the first Games there weren't as many. Basically, it was a javelin and archery competition. A lot of people find archery surprising, because they often think that the Games started with more common disciplines such as wheelchair racing or discus throwing.

Sonia: Who had the idea to start an Olympic Games event for people with physical disabilities?

Vikram: It was Dr Ludwig Guttman who organised the first Games for his patients. The use of sport in his treatment of spinal injuries was quite revolutionary for that time. He believed that sport could make his patients' lives much better and he enjoyed watching them getting involved. As a result of these Games, his patients became more competitive and independent in their lives once they left the clinic. The patients were already learning a lot of skills, but these didn't seem to have the same impact that the competitive sports had, so the Games soon became an event that was held annually.

Sonia: How did this event grow in popularity?

Vikram: Well, it was Dr Guttman's dream to make the Stoke Mandeville Games into an international event. This became a reality 12 years later in 1960 when the first Paralympic Games were held in Italy. Compared to their humble beginnings at the Stoke Mandeville hospital, the Games in 1960 hosted 400 athletes from 23 countries. It was quite an achievement if you compare it with the first Summer Olympics which only hosted 14 countries. However, the first Winter Paralympic Games were held in Sweden in 1976 with just 12 countries competing. Originally, the participants were just wheelchair users.

Sonia: Any other interesting facts about the Paralympics?

Vikram: There are plenty, Sonia. The Games were not officially called the Paralympics until quite recently. The term was first used in Seoul in 1988. In 1976 the Games expanded in order to include athletes with other disabilities. Soon after, athletes with blindness and amputees started participating in the Games. At present, we have six major categories of athletes from 145 different countries at the Paralympics. However, athletes can move to a different category or classification as they grow older.

Sonia: Do the Olympic and Paralympic Games always happen at the same time?

Vikram: Well, at first, the Olympic and Paralympic Games were held at different times and venues. That changed in 1988 for the Summer Games and in 1992 for the Winter Games. Since then, both sets of Games have been held within two weeks of each other at the same venue. This wasn't always the case in the past. For example, in 1968 the Olympic Games were held in Mexico and the Paralympics took place in Israel.

Sonia: I heard that the Games in Atlanta played an important role in the Games' history.

Vikram: Since the beginning we've seen more and more people go to see the Paralympics live. And with each Games we've seen new sports being added and more and more sportsmen and sportswomen from all over the world competing in the Games, so it came as no surprise that with such popularity, when the Games were held in Atlanta, the broadcasting rights were bought by TV companies, something that had never happened before.

Sonia: And what about the state of the Paralympic Games today?

Vikram: Sadly, Dr Guttmann died in 1980. However, his legacy lives on. He had a vision for sport to be much more than just an activity for his patients to help them with their rehabilitation, and I think he succeeded. The fact that the Paralympics have become the second biggest sporting event in the world after the Summer Olympics is impressive. The determination of the athletes should be an inspiration to all of us.

Sonia: Well, thank you very much for this interview. It was very uplifting.

Vikram: It's a pleasure.

Transcript 15 (track 16)

Speaker 1:
I was given this for my birthday. I was really surprised at first because I never asked for one. It has a 32-gigabyte memory so I could upload quite a few songs, if I knew how. I know it's a very useful device and there were instructions, but I'm not very good with technology. I use gadgets a lot, but setting up things or following instructions is not something I'm good at. I'd been trying to make it work for ages but, in the end, I lost patience and put it on the table beside my bed. I was cross with myself and put off by not knowing how to use it and, unless my cousin helps me, I don't think I'll ever use it.

Speaker 2:
When I started university, I promised myself that I'd learn to cook. I didn't want to end up going out every night and eating junk food. I also didn't want to eat ready meals, like most of my friends. I was living in a small bedsit, so buying a cooker would have been impractical. Also, my mum was a bit scared that I might burn the place down with a normal cooker, and she suggested buying this instead. I thought it was a good compromise. When I started cooking, my friends were excited, but I soon realised its limitations. It was simple to operate for reheating food, but not for serious cooking. Nothing I cooked in it came out crisp. It was a real let-down.

Speaker 3:
I love reading and I'd been dreaming of having one of these ever since they first came out. When I go on holiday, I really enjoy reading a lot. Sometimes I finish five novels in a week. But you can imagine that taking five with you when travelling by plane is a bit impractical. So I was really thrilled when I got one of the latest models two years ago. You might say, it's not the same as reading a real one, but I don't mind in the slightest. Now everywhere I go, it comes with me in my handbag.

Speaker 4:
I don't really like cleaning. I always want efficient equipment so that I can quickly finish the job but with a good result. I bought this new model and tried it straight away. It really did a good job. It wasn't even on full power, but the carpets all looked so clean. We have a pet and there are often a lot of pet hairs on the carpet, but I must say it got rid of all of them. I was so pleased that I even wrote a customer review and gave it five stars so people who are frustrated with their old ones can get this new model.

Speaker 5:

My grandson bought one for me because he wants me to be able to contact him at any time and he was so excited about the idea. He's living away this year and I miss him a lot. I wanted to give it a go, but now I keep it switched off for most of the time because I read an article that too much exposure is harmful. I'm also worried that I may press the wrong button and phone someone by mistake, which would be really embarrassing.

Speaker 6:

I've had these for a month, but I still struggle when I'm trying to put them in each morning. I'm not giving up though because they're really practical and discreet. Even though it's still tricky for me to use them, I'm not disappointed. My optician told me this might happen and I'm sure it'll get easier in the long run. I'm even thinking of getting a spare pair in a different colour once I've got used to these ones.

Transcript 16 (track 17)

Recording 1
Female student: Hi Tiago. How are you doing? I haven't seen you for ages.

Tiago: Not too bad. I've been really busy lately.

Female student: Yes, I know what you mean. The same here. What do you think about the new IGCSE exams? Do you think they're more difficult than the old ones?

Tiago: We'll have to wait and see. Only time will tell.

Recording 2
Male student: I've heard that the maths exam was really difficult.

Female student: Yes, it was really tough.

Male student: Do you think you'll pass?

Female student: I'd rather not talk about it, if you don't mind.

Recording 3
Female student: Fancy coming to my birthday party?

Male student: Yes, that would be cool, but I've never been to your place. How do I get there?

Female student: It's very simple. When you get to the city centre, you get on the 22 bus and get off outside the new ice rink. Then you take the first left and after about 500 metres you take the third right. Simple.

Male student: Sorry, you've lost me.

Recording 4
Male student: Hey, Jasmine. Great to see you! I was wondering if you could help me out.

Jasmine: What is it?

Male student: I have to prepare for this quiz on Saturday. It's about endangered animals from our country. I've been racking my brains to think of some endangered animals, but so far I've only thought of five. Can you help?

Jasmine: Let me see … Hmmm. Sorry, nothing springs to mind.

Transcript 17 (track 18)

1 Sorry, I'm not <u>following</u>.

2 Sorry, I didn't quite <u>catch</u> that.

3 It's <u>too</u> early to say.

4 Sorry, how do you <u>mean</u>?

5 Sorry, my mind's gone <u>completely</u> blank.

Transcript 18 (track 19)

Good morning and thank you all for coming today. The topic of today's talk is endangered animals. I would like to cover several points. I'd like to share some shocking statistics with you and the most common reasons why some species are disappearing. However, I don't want you to leave the talk feeling depressed, so I'm also going to mention the efforts people round the world are making to save our endangered animals, and finally, one success story too.

Endangered species are classified by the numbers remaining in the wild, ranging from the most extreme to the least extreme cases. The most critical category is 'critically endangered' followed by 'endangered' and then 'vulnerable' species. There is one more category called 'extinct in the wild'. These species are only found in captivity because there are no surviving animals in the wild.

We decide on the category depending on how many animals there are remaining. For example, for the critically endangered group there are fewer than 250 fully-grown animals left, followed by 2500 or fewer for the endangered category, and 10 000 or fewer for the vulnerable species. We also keep statistics about the future predictions for these species. If nothing radical is done, it is now predicted that 50 per cent of the remaining population of endangered animals will be lost forever in the next 10 years. This is a massive increase on the prediction from 20 years ago when experts predicted that 20 per cent of the animals would disappear. As you can see the situation is critical.

The most common reason for a species to become endangered is an extreme change to their natural habitat. This might be related, indirectly, to global warming, or to more specific human activities, such as deforestation, which directly damage the environment where the animals live. Other reasons for the decline in numbers are the hunting and poaching of animals. I'd like to mention one more reason, one that we tend to forget. It is the non-native species that are introduced by humans to a new habitat. These 'alien' species then become competition to the native species, which often proves fatal for the native species because the natural balance of the food chain is disturbed.

For a long time, experts have been working relentlessly to save as many endangered animals as possible. Unfortunately, this has always been done in small numbers only. But in more recent years, some famous people have become involved and use their names to raise awareness all around the world. They have also donated their money to fund various projects. Leonardo DiCaprio, for example, is someone who has become involved in the fight to save the remaining population of tigers. He has spoken publicly about the problem and has also donated some of his money to the cause. Speaking of tigers, I also have to mention one of India's attempts to save these beautiful animals. Bhagani is one of the four villages in the Sariska National Park that is set to relocate elsewhere, so that the place can be turned into a haven for tigers. It is the kind of habitat they need to breed and live undisturbed.

Before I finish my talk today, I would like to tell you about one success story. It's the story of the American Bald Eagle. Back in the 1960s there were fewer than 400 of these birds in the United States. To raise awareness of the issue, whole communities were involved. Not just the adults, children too. At schools there were 'Eagle days' during which children would learn more about these birds, enter competitions in writing stories and compose songs about them. In certain areas volunteers would keep watch and make a note of how many eagles they had spotted and where. This data was then passed on to conservationists, who made sure that nests in these areas were protected from poachers. Nowadays, the numbers are up to 10 000 thanks to the effort made by all these people, and this impressive bird has been taken off the endangered list. Let us hope that this success story will be repeated many times from now on and we'll be able to save most of our endangered species.

Does anyone have any questions …

Transcript 19 (track 20)

Speaker 1:
I really admire this person. Every time I feel that things are really difficult and it's almost impossible to think of a solution to my problems, I go and read his autobiography. This person achieved a lot, simply because he never gave up. There were times in his life when everything seemed lost and he had to start from scratch again. Many other people would have just given up, but not him. He just kept going. The task he set for himself was to free his country, so not an easy thing to do. He was also brave – but, above all, his greatest quality was the determination to see his dream come true.

Speaker 2:
One day I read an article about an extraordinary woman who sailed round the world on her own. At first you might think that it's just a great adventure and the only things you need are confidence and a lot of experience. You couldn't be more wrong. This woman had to put up with all sorts of problems. Let's take the weather for example. When you encounter a bad storm on land, you can look for shelter. When this happens at sea, no matter how scary this is, you have to keep your cool. There is no place to hide, no place to run. Plus, there's no one to talk to, no one to ask for advice. You're on your own and you need a lot of courage.

Speaker 3:

I first heard about this woman when I was a small child so I didn't pay much attention then. When I was a teenager, I saw a documentary about her and I thought her work for humanity was worth following. I can't help but respect her for all her achievements. She gave up all her material comfort to help others and put their needs before hers. Some of her friends questioned her decision saying it wasn't wise, but I think we need to hear about people like her more often in our material world. We forget that life is not all about material possessions. She inspired me so much that I've taken up a voluntary job for one of our local charities helping children from disadvantaged backgrounds with their education.

Speaker 4:

A lot of people my age look up to someone famous, but I have to say that we often forget about the ordinary people and the people closest to us. I really respect my grandfather. His life hasn't been easy. I guess it has taught him a lot of valuable lessons and that's why he always has an answer to every problem or question. No matter what I ask him about, he gives me good advice based on his own experience and this has helped me get through my own problems. I can't imagine what I would do without him. I don't think we appreciate this amazing source of knowledge and information enough and that's a shame.

Speaker 5:

We were never bored with him. When my brother and I were little, we used to go for long walks in the forest with our dad. He would always come up with extraordinary stories about the wildlife. Not everyone was so patient to listen to his fantasies though. Mum would just say that he should take life more seriously. But we loved his stories. When we grew up, I always thought it would be a shame if these stories got forgotten so I encouraged him to write them down. We had such nice evenings getting together and trying to remember all his stories. It reminded us of when we were little again. We were all so pleased when his book of children's stories got published last year. It made us really proud of him.

Speaker 6:

I've been thinking long and hard and I think the person I look up to most is my mum. It's very easy to forget how hard our mums work. They often juggle two or even more jobs. My mum had to look after the four of us and we weren't little angels. I don't understand how she managed to be so calm when we were naughty. She would have just said, 'I'm very disappointed with you'. However, she always encouraged us to be self-confident. On top of everything, she had a job in the local nursery school, so she had even more children to look after. She never complained. I don't know how she did it.

Acknowledgements

The author and publishers acknowledge the following sources of copyright material and are grateful for the permissions granted. While every effort has been made, it has not always been possible to identify the sources of all the material used, or to trace all copyright holders. If any omissions are brought to our notice, we will be happy to include the appropriate acknowledgements on reprinting.

Text

p3 News Limited / News CorpAustraliahttp://www.news.com.au/travel/travel-updates/worlds-weirdest-welcomings/story-e6frfq80-1226005607767p18 www.festivalpig.com/p30 Grace Murano, Oddee.com, www.oddee.com p73 www.indians.orghttp://www.indians.org/articles/totem-poles.htmlp73 Courtesy of Silk & Stone, www.silknstone.com p80 Kathryn Vercillo, www.crochetconcupiscence.com p119 Roy D'Silva/Buzzle.com p128 www.wisegeek.com

Images

Cover Chad Ehlers/The Image Bank/Getty Images;p1 Sergey Nivens / Shutterstock; p2tl Blaine Harrington / Getty Images; p2tc Image Source / Getty Images; p2tr Odua Images / Shutterstock; p2bl Rawpixel / Shutterstock; p2bc XiXinXing / Shutterstock; p2br © Paul Kingsley / Alamy; p12 (thief) AmmentorpPhotography / Shutterstock; p12 (phone) nyul / Thinkstock; p12 (eating) Greg Ceo / Getty Images; p12 (tourists) Razvan / Thinkstock; p12 (handshake) Jupiterimages / Shutterstock; p12 (shoes) STOCK4B-RF / Getty Images; p12 (queue) Mitchell Funk / Getty Images; p16 JeremyRichards / Shutterstock; p17tl Tayseer AL-Hamad / Getty Images; p17tr Robert Frerck / Getty Images; p17bl Peter Unger / Getty Images; p17br © JEON HEON-KYUN/epa/Corbis; p19 © David Bathgate/Corbis; p23 CelsoPupo / Shutterstock; p24 1eyeshut / Shutterstock; p28 RIRF Stock / Shutterstock; p29l Marques / Shutterstock; p29r LaurensT / Shutterstock; p30 Alex Treadway / Getty Images; p31 Michal Ninger / Shutterstock; p35l Sam DCruz / Shutterstock; p35c Travelpix Ltd / Getty Images; p35r 1000 Words / Shutterstock; p35b SlavkoSereda / Shutterstock; p36l Ron Watts / Getty Images; p36c Rich Carey / Shutterstock; p36r Damien Polegato / Getty Images; p38 Dimitri Vervitsiotis / Getty Images; p42 Neo Edmund / Shutterstock; p43 John Lamb / Getty Images; p44 NASA/SCIENCE PHOTO LIBRARY; p50 NASA/SCIENCE PHOTO LIBRARY; p58 enciktat / Shutterstock; p59l © Tetra Images / Alamy; p59r Brendan O'Sullivan / Getty Images; p63 Terry Williams / Getty Images; p64 Chris Schmidt / Getty Images; p68t Alexander Nicholson / Getty Images; p68c Monkey Business Images / Shutterstock; p68b © Blend Images / Alamy; p71 Xiaojiao Wang / Shutterstock; p72tl Eric Limon / Shutterstock; p72tc © Hemis / Alamy; p72tr dedoma / Shutterstock; p72bl DEA PICTURE LIBRARY / Getty Images; p72bc 2009fotofriends / Shutterstock; p72br NY-P/Shutterstock; p76 mimagephotography / Shutterstock; p79 twospeeds / Shutterstock; p80 KidStock / Getty Images; p82l olyniteowl / Getty Images; p82cl Monkey Business Images / Shutterstock; p82cr BlueOrange Studio / Shutterstock; p82r © Design Pics Inc / Alamy; p84 Lonely Planet / Getty Images; p85t © Blend Images / Alamy; p85b moodboard / Thinkstock; p86 john j. klaiberjr / Shutterstock; p87tl Marcio Eugenio / Shutterstock; p87tcl ALEKSI TUOMOLA / Getty Images; p87tcr Sorbis / Shutterstock; p87tr Will Hughes / Shutterstock; p87bl WebSubstance / Getty Images; p87bc maratr / Shutterstock; p87br AFP/ Getty Images; p92 Chris M. Rogers / Getty Images; p93t David Madison / Getty Images; p93b © PCN/Corbis; p97 aerogondo2 / Shutterstock; p101 DenisKlimov / Shutterstock; p102tl Christian Delbert / Shutterstock; p102tcl Syda Productions / Shutterstock; p102tcr © BlueBell / Alamy; p102tr wavebreakmedia /

Shutterstock; p102bl © ArtBabii / Alamy; p102bc © milos luzanin / Alamy; p102br Peter Dazeley / Getty Images; p104 Christina Reichl Photography / Getty Images; p106 © Tetra Images / Alamy; p108 Flying Colours Ltd / Getty Images; p112 Monkey Business Images / Shutterstock; p113 altrendo images / Getty Images; p116 Mark Bridger / Shutterstock; p117tr Soren Egeberg Photography / Shutterstock; p117tc Mike Price / Shutterstock; p117tr Denise Allison Coyle / Shutterstock; p117bl SCIEPRO / Getty Images; p117bcl Chris Fourie / Shutterstock; p117bcr Chris Gardiner / Shutterstock; p117br Hung Chung Chih / Shutterstock; p118 Nick Biemans / Shutterstock; p122 © Blue Jean Images / Alamy; p124 dmvphotos / Shutterstock; p125r David Woodfall / Getty Images; p125c Tui De Roy / Getty Images; p125r Lori Epstein / Getty Images; p126 PhillipRubinop127 AFP/ Getty Images; p132 © Hongqi Zhang / Alamy; p133tl © ClassicStock / Alamy; p133tcl © Adria Diane Hughes/Demotix/Corbis; p133tcr © Tim Wimborne/Reuters/Corbis; p133tr cinemafestival / Shutterstock; p133bl © Corbis; p133bcl © Bettmann/Corbis; p133bcr © Ali Imam/Reuters/Corbis; p133br s_bukley / Shutterstock; p134 © Corbis; p137 Paul Bradbury / Getty Images; p138 David Malan / Getty Images; p140tl Corepics VOF / Shutterstock; p140tc Courtney Keating / Getty Images; p140tr photogl / Shutterstock; p140bl wongyuliang / Shutterstock; p140br Dan Kitwood / Getty Images; p143 Hill Street Studios / Getty Images